Reading & Writing With Picture Books

Grade 2

Table of Contents

www.themailbox.com

©2003 by THE EDUCATION CENTER, INC.
All rights reserved.
ISBN# 1-56234-531-1

Manufactured in the United States
10 9 8 7 6 5 4 3 2 1

Reading & Writing With Picture Books

Using Literature to Reinforce Essential Skills

Reading & Writing With Picture Books provides a solid, kid-pleasing foundation for your reading and writing instruction! Literature can open up new worlds for students and can be used to teach a variety of reading and writing skills and strategies. In *Reading & Writing With Picture Books,* you'll find the inspiration and information you need to set up meaningful reading and writing experiences that reinforce essential literacy skills and promote the use of reading comprehension strategies.

Seven Benefits of Using the Activities in This Book

1. When children hear stories read aloud as suggested throughout this book, they are freed from the word-identification tasks involved in independent reading and can **devote more attention to comprehending the stories** using their prior knowledge.
2. Reading or listening to stories, writing in response to them, and getting involved in discussions **enhance children's abilities to understand the things they read.**
3. Reading nurtures writing performance. Writing nurtures reading skills. Relating reading and writing experiences as the activities in this book suggest **prompts growth in both areas,** while also positively influencing students' **thinking skills.**
4. When children hear the same story read aloud several times (as is suggested in this book), they begin to notice things they didn't notice during the first reading. Rereading helps students **understand how the author shaped the story** and gives them **ideas to use in their own writing.**
5. Conversations about stories **provide opportunities to model the use of reading strategies**—such as making connections, visualizing, and inferring—and to **assess which reading strategies children are using and how effectively they are applying them.**
6. When children write in response to reading, they use what they know about reading and writing in ways that are personally important and **meaningful.**
7. The types of goal-oriented and engaging activities included in this book also help children **view reading and writing as purposeful, pleasant experiences and increase their interest in literacy activities.**

Before Reading

- Activate prior knowledge by discussing with students what they know about the picture book's subject matter.
- Set a purpose for reading by encouraging students to predict what will happen or have them listen with a specific purpose in mind.
- Alert students to any new or unfamiliar vocabulary that appears in the text.

During Reading

- Set an example for students and make the text more engaging by reading with emotion and excitement.
- Talk aloud about what you're reading and what you're thinking about as you read. Make predictions and summarize events as you go. Think aloud by verbalizing the questions you have about the text. Also mention what you're inferring and what you're visualizing. Encourage students to use these strategies too.

After Reading

- Lead students in a discussion of the story. Then follow up with one or more of the activities in *Reading & Writing With Picture Books*!

Included in This Book

Reading & Writing With Picture Books includes 12 units. In each unit, a different high-quality literature selection is used as the starting point for a collection of skill-based reading and writing activities. The format of this practical reference allows you to choose featured books and accompanying activities based on your students' needs and interests. Within each unit, you'll find the following elements:

book summary	**center**
reading activities	**reproducibles**
writing activities	**icons**
skills information	

Each **book summary** gives you an overview of the book. Three **reading activities** enhance your students' understanding of specific, grade-appropriate reading skills and strategies. Three **writing activities** help students improve their writing skills while reflecting on the story and creating written responses related to it. A featured **skill or strategy** is highlighted above each activity title, making this an at-a-glance resource for preparing lesson plans. In addition, reading and writing skills grids can be found on pages 78 and 79 to use as quick and easy references. One **center** activity that highlights a reading or writing skill is provided in each unit. You'll also find **reproducibles** that can be used to enhance specific activities, to provide individual practice, or to give quick assessments of understanding. Each reading, writing, and center idea is clearly marked with an easy-to-read **icon.**

Reading & Writing With Picture Books

Managing Editor: Hope H. Taylor
Editor at Large: Diane Badden
Staff Editors: Denine T. Carter, Kelli L. Gowdy
Contributing Writers: Peggy Morin Bruno, Vicki Dabrowka, Cynthia Holcomb, Natalie Hughes-Tanner, Starin Lewis, Diane F. McGraw, Kimberly Minafo
Copy Editors: Karen Brewer Grossman, Amy Kirtley-Hill, Karen L. Mayworth, Debbie Shoffner
Cover Artist: Nick Greenwood
Art Coordinator: Clevell Harris
Artists: Pam Crane, Theresa Lewis Goode, Nick Greenwood, Clevell Harris, Ivy L. Koonce, Sheila Krill, Clint Moore, Greg D. Rieves, Rebecca Saunders, Barry Slate, Donna K. Teal
Typesetters: Lynette Dickerson, Mark Rainey

President, The Mailbox Book Company™: Joseph C. Bucci
Director of Book Planning and Development: Chris Poindexter
Book Development Managers: Cayce Guiliano, Elizabeth H. Lindsay, Thad McLaurin, Susan Walker
Curriculum Director: Karen P. Shelton
Traffic Manager: Lisa K. Pitts
Librarian: Dorothy C. McKinney
Editorial and Freelance Management: Karen A. Brudnak
Editorial Training: Irving P. Crump
Editorial Assistants: Hope Rodgers, Jan E. Witcher

Tacky the Penguin

Written by Helen Lester
Illustrated by Lynn Munsinger

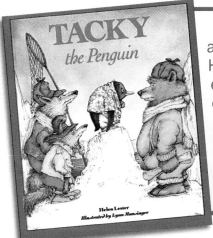

Tacky the Penguin is certainly not your average penguin. His singing is too loud. He loves to make cannonball splashes. He even dresses differently from his dignified companions. But when a pack of rough and tough hunters comes thumping across the ice, Tacky holds his own. After the penguin's unusual behavior frightens the puzzled pack away, Tacky's pals decide that his unique qualities make him a pretty special friend!

Conflict and resolution

Penguin Problems

Though Tacky appears oblivious to his oddities, his unusual behavior often causes trouble for his friends. Before reading the book aloud, draw and label a chart on the chalkboard as shown. Instruct students to listen for examples of Tacky's unusual behavior as you read the book aloud. In addition, encourage them to search the illustrations for clues about Tacky's actions as well as his companions' reactions to them. As each example is pointed out, list it in the first column.

Next, guide students in a discussion of the trouble each situation may cause for the other penguins. Prompt their thinking by asking questions such as the following: Why do you think Tacky's behavior bothers the other penguins? How do you think Tacky's friends treat him differently? How do you think this makes Tacky feel? In the second column, record students' ideas about the problems each of Tacky's behaviors may cause.

After reading the book, have students think about each of Tacky's behaviors, in turn, and discuss how it contributes to the story's solution *(scaring the hunters away).* Guide them to conclude that Tacky's odd nature leads to his heroic actions. For an esteem-building wrap-up, prompt students to share how their own unique qualities can have positive effects on their everyday situations.

Tacky's Behavior	Problem
Tacky's marching is clumsy.	The other penguins don't want to march near Tacky. He bumps into them!

Unlocking New Vocabulary

Help students breeze through new vocabulary with this activity! Give each of several student volunteers an index card on which you have written one of the words below. Have the child listen for his assigned word as you reread the book aloud. Have him raise his hand when he hears his word. At that point, stop, read the passage containing the word again, and then have students discuss the word's meaning. After completing the activity, have each student complete a copy of page 9 for further vocabulary review.

chanting	companions
fright	odd
blared	greeted
growled	hearty
puzzled	graceful
dreadfully	thump

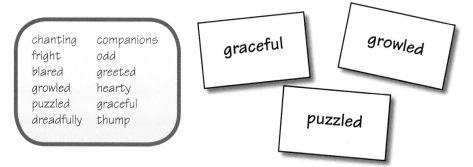

graceful

growled

puzzled

Making Sense of Setting

Give students a sense of setting by encouraging them to use their five senses! Begin by gathering students and revisiting the book's icy illustrations. Invite students to speculate about where the story might take place. Then provide each child with a sheet of drawing paper. After she draws a small picture of Tacky in the middle of the paper, have her draw and label a web space for each of the five senses as shown. Next, ask her to imagine what Tacky might see, hear, feel, smell, and taste in his home. Tell her to record her thoughts on the web. Provide time for students to share their completed pages with the class.

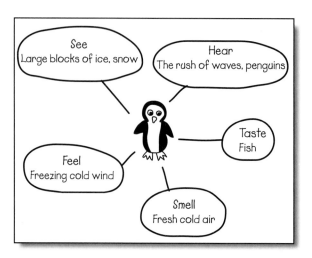

See
Large blocks of ice, snow

Hear
The rush of waves, penguins

Taste
Fish

Feel
Freezing cold wind

Smell
Fresh cold air

Tacky's True Traits

Students are sure to agree—Tacky is quite a character! But there's more to this unparalleled penguin than meets the eye. Remind students that Tacky's obvious character traits, such as the way he dresses and his loud nature, make him seem odd to his companions. Point out that these traits tell only part of the story and that Tacky's most important qualities are harder to see.

Next, give one copy of page 10 to each student. Tell him to cut out the penguin pattern along the solid lines and then fold in the wings as shown. On the outside of each wing, have him write words or phrases that describe Tacky's outward appearance and behavior. Then instruct him to unfold the wings and, on the lines provided, write qualities about Tacky that are revealed when the hunters arrive. Direct the student to color the penguin, being careful to avoid his writing. Encourage students to share their projects with the class, offering explanations for the qualities they chose. Display the penguin projects on a bulletin board titled "The Truth About Tacky."

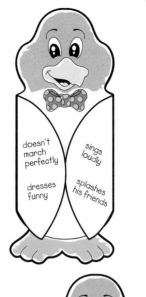

Who's Who?

This sensational center helps students sort out the differences between Tacky and his friends. To create two heading strips, label one sentence strip "Tacky" and a second strip "Other Penguins." Next, program each of several index cards with a different word from the list on this page. To make the center self-checking, color-code the back of the cards and sentence strips accordingly. Place the heading strips, index cards, writing paper, pencils, and a copy of the book at a center.

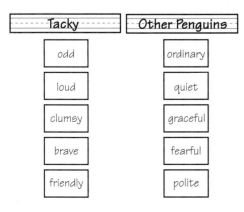

Instruct each student to arrange the heading strips on the work surface and then sort the cards by placing each one below the appropriate headings. Next, tell the student to refer to the cards as he writes a short paragraph comparing Tacky to the other penguins. Now that's getting character traits in order!

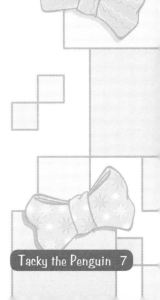

Tracking Down Adjectives

Send students on a hunt for adjectives! Remind students that an adjective is a word that describes a person, place, or thing. Next, read aloud the two-page spread that introduces the hunters. Ask student volunteers to name the two adjectives that describe the hunters (rough and tough). Then challenge youngsters to brainstorm other words that describe the hunters, such as *mean, greedy,* or *scary.*

To continue the hunt, give each child a sheet of writing paper. Challenge the child to list the adjectives he hears and the noun each describes as you reread the book aloud. Pause at the end of each page to allow time for students to record their answers. To wrap up the activity, have each child write five sentences. Direct him to use one of his listed word pairs in each sentence.

icy land
odd bird
hearty slap
graceful divers
splashy cannonballs

Tacky Continued

Guide students into taking Tacky on another adventure! As a class, brainstorm ideas for another problem that Tacky and his companions could face, such as a polar bear invasion, a blizzard, or a bow tie thief. List students' ideas on the board. Then have each child use one of the listed ideas to draft a story with a clear beginning, middle, and end.

To publish his work, have the student trim an 8½" x 11" sheet of writing paper into an oval. Direct him to copy his story on the resulting shape and remind him to title and sign his work. Next, tell the student to round the corners of a 9" x 12" sheet of black construction paper to create a penguin body. Then have him staple his story onto the body cutout. Instruct him to cut out eyes, a nose, wings, and feet from construction paper scraps and then glue the body parts into place. Encourage students to share their terrific Tacky stories with the class!

Piecing Together New Words

Read each sentence. Write the letter of the correct
   word from the box.
To assemble the puzzle, cut out the boxes below.
Match the letter on each box to the number of its
   sentence.
Glue the pieces in place.

_____ 1. Tacky shares a home with his five penguin _____.

_____ 2. Tacky is an _____ bird.

_____ 3. Tacky greets his friends with a _____ slap on the
   back.

_____ 4. The other penguins are _____ divers.

_____ 5. The penguins hear the hunters _____ as they
   come closer.

_____ 6. "What's happening?" _____ Tacky loudly.

_____ 7. The hunters are _____ by Tacky's strange
   behavior.

_____ 8. Tacky begins singing as _____ as he can.

a. puzzled

b. dreadfully

c. odd

d. hearty

e. companions

f. blared

g. chanting

h. graceful

7	1	8	4
2	3	6	5

Note to the teacher: Use with "Unlocking New Vocabulary" on page 6.

9

Penguin Pattern

Use with "Tacky's True Traits" on page 7.

Tacky is

_____

_____

_____

_____

Bringing the Rain to Kapiti Plain

Retold by Verna Aardema
Illustrated by Beatriz Vidal

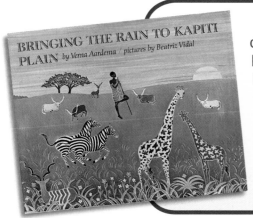

The life of a herdsman on the African plain has its challenges! On Kapiti Plain, Ki-pat becomes concerned as he watches his cattle and the earth suffering from a lack of rain. Finally, he takes matters into his own hands and brings the rain to his beloved plain. Students will enjoy the rhythmic and poetic patterns Aardema uses to bring this cumulative tale to life!

Activating prior knowledge

What Is It About Rain?

Before your students take a literary trek to the African plains, find out what they already know about rain. On the board, create a large three-columned chart headed like the one shown. Direct students' attention to each column, have them brainstorm a list of answers to each question, and write their answers in the corresponding column.

After completing the chart, explain to students that they will be studying a book about a man who experiences a drought, or a period with no rain. As you read the book aloud, pause on each page and invite students to use what they know about rain to predict what will happen next.

What does rain do?	What happens when there's no rain?	Where does rain come from?
• Rain gives plants water. • Rain fills rivers. • Rain washes things clean.	• Plants die. • Rivers dry up. • Things become dusty and dry.	• Rain falls from the clouds.

Rhythmic Raindrop Reading

A sparkling prediction lesson starts with this glittery raindrop wand. To make the wand, trim two 4" x 5" blue construction paper rectangles into raindrop shapes. Glue one shape on either side of the same end of a ruler as shown. If desired, use glue and glitter to decorate the wand.

To prepare for the lesson, copy several verses from the book onto chart paper. Use a sticky note to cover the word at the end of each fourth line as shown. Next, gather students around the chart and instruct them to read aloud as you use the wand to point to each word in turn. At the end of each fourth line, pause at the sticky note and have different student volunteers each provide a suggestion for the missing word(s) and then explain his choice. Continue in this manner as time allows.

"This is Ki-pat,
    who watched his herd
As he stood on one leg,
    like the big stork   ;"

Piecing Together the Plain

The order of events is key to unleashing the rain cloud over Kapiti Plain. Use this sentence-writing activity to help students write about and then sequence those events. After a shared reading of *Bringing the Rain to Kapiti Plain,* give one copy of page 15 to each child. Instruct the child to study each picture and then write a complete sentence describing the events in the picture. Remind the child to include a subject and predicate in his sentence. In addition, encourage him to use proper capitalization and punctuation.

Next, have the child color and then cut apart the pages. Instruct him to read each event and place the pages in sequential order. Help him stack his pages and then staple them to form a small booklet. Finally, invite the child to use his booklet to retell the story to his family.

When the rain stops, the cows are hungry.

The eagle drops feather.

Ki-Pat makes an arrow.

Ki-Pat shoots the arrow at the cloud.

The rain falls.

Now little Ki-Pat watches the herd.

Feathery Effects

Finding the cause and effect in this rainy weather story provides the perfect inspiration for compound-sentence writing! Prepare a large feather-shaped cutout (see sample). Draw writing lines on either side of the feather's shaft and then label the two columns as shown. Program the "Effects" column with story events, written as complete sentences, that can be traced to specific causes.

Have a student volunteer read one event aloud. Ask students to name the cause of the event and then write it as a complete sentence in the "Causes" column. Continue in this manner until each cause is listed.

Next, demonstrate how to use words such as *since, so,* and *because* to combine two sentences into one compound sentence. For example, recite sentences such as "The rains are late so the creatures migrate" and "The grass is brown and dead because it needs rain." Give each child a sheet of colorful construction paper and have him trim it into a feather shape. Instruct him to refer to the cause-and-effect list as he writes one compound sentence on one side of his cutout. Then have him write a second sentence on the back of the cutout.

Causes	Effects
The rains and late.	The creatures migrate.
It needs rain.	The grass is brown and dead.
The cows are hungry and dry.	The cows moo for rain.

The cows moo for rain because they are hungry and dry.

Rainy Day Sentences

The forecast calls for learning when students visit this cloudy sentence center! Prepare ten gray raindrop-shaped cutouts and then program each one with a different sentence part as shown. Laminate the cutouts and then place them in a center along with writing paper and pencils. In addition, cover a six-sided die with masking tape and use a permanent marker to program each side with one of the following ending punctuation marks: period, question mark, or exclamation point. Display the die in the center.

Each student finds a match for each raindrop. Next, she rolls the die and then uses the punctuation mark rolled and the words from one raindrop pair to write a sentence on her paper. Instruct her to add extra words to make the sentences complete as necessary, and remind her to capitalize the first letter. Have her continue in this manner until she has written a sentence for each raindrop pair.

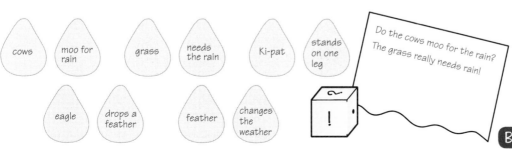

cows

moo for rain

grass

needs the rain

Ki-pat

stands on one leg

eagle

drops a feather

feather

changes the weather

Do the cows moo for the rain? The grass really needs rain!

Antonym Analysis

A discussion of Kapiti Plain's transformation from a dry, brown place to a lush, green pasture provides the perfect springboard for this antonym game! After reading aloud *Bringing the Rain to Kapiti Plain,* ask students to name adjectives that describe the plain before the rain, such as *dry* and *vacant,* as you list their ideas on the board. Then have them suggest adjectives that describe the plain after the rain, such as *wet* and *populated,* and list those on the board. Point out pairs of words that are antonyms, such as *wet* and *dry.*

To extend the lesson, play this antonym bingo game. Program 16 two-inch construction paper squares each with one of the antonyms listed on this page. Place the squares in a container. Next, give each student a copy of page 16 and 16 game markers. Instruct him to cut along the dotted line and then cut apart the game cards. Have him randomly glue the cards onto the gameboard.

To play a round, take a card from the container and read the word aloud. Have each student place a game marker on a board space that contains an antonym of the word. Continue playing until one student has four markers in a diagonal, vertical, or horizontal row and calls out, "Kapiti!" Verify that his words are antonyms of words called and then have students clear their boards for another round.

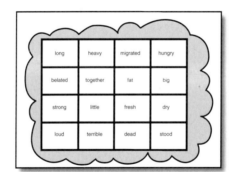

Antonyms for Construction Paper Squares	Gameboard Words
stale	fresh
early	belated
settled	migrated
good	terrible
light	heavy
alive	dead
small	big
wet	dry
sat	stood
apart	together
short	long
weak	strong
quiet	loud
thin	fat
large	little
full	hungry

Showers of Story Starters

Ki-Pat's ingenuity brings the rain to the plain. Give your students the opportunity to find their own creative solutions with this writing activity. To prepare, program several raindrop-shaped cutouts each with a different rhyming story title, such as "Bringing the Snow to Mexico," "Bringing the Light Into the Night," and "Bringing the Sun to Washington." Display the cutouts on a wall above an umbrella-shaped cutout and title the display "Showers of Story Starters." Direct each child to study the raindrops, choose one title, and draft a story for the title.

To publish her story, direct the child to print a clean copy on writing paper. Then have her mount the writing paper onto a large raindrop-shaped cutout. Invite each child to read her story aloud and then arrange the cutouts on a bulletin board titled "Showers of Solutions."

©The Education Center, Inc. • *Reading & Writing With Picture Books* • TEC1791

Gameboard and Game Cards

Use with "Antonym Analysis" on page 14.

belated	dead	together	fat
migrated	big	long	little
terrible	dry	strong	hungry
heavy	stood	loud	fresh

Frog and Toad Are Friends

Written and illustrated by Arnold Lobel

In this timeless 1971 Caldecott Honor Book, Frog and Toad help each other cope with situations that are sure to sound familiar. Children will sympathize with Frog when he is not feeling well. They will understand how Toad feels when people laugh at him. And who can't relate to Toad's longing to receive mail? *Frog and Toad Are Friends* is a collection of simple stories about two best friends who share adventures and care for each other in times of trouble.

Character study

Opposites Attract

Youngsters will flip over character analysis with this charming interactive activity! Provide one tagboard copy of page 21 for each child. Instruct the child to color and cut out both characters and then glue the cutouts back-to-back.

Next, point out that sometimes, as with Frog and Toad, characters that are very different are good friends. Share *Frog and Toad Are Friends* with the class. Then invite volunteers to share some examples of Frog and Toad's differences. For example, during the search for Toad's lost button, Toad loses his temper, whereas Frog remains patient. Then recite a quote made by Frog or Toad, such as "Spring is a beautiful time of year" or "I am going back to bed until May." Direct each student to decide which character would be most likely to have said the quote and hold up the appropriate side of his character cutout. Scan the room to confirm students' answers before reciting another quote. Continue in this manner as time allows. To follow up, have each student write three sentences that describe each character in the box on the appropriate side of the cutout. What characters!

Button Lineup

The search for a great sequencing lesson ends at this event-filled center! Make a class supply of the story event circles on page 22 and display them in the center. In addition, place a copy of the book, a supply of 12-inch white construction paper squares, scissors, glue, and crayons in the center.

Each visitor to the center rereads "A Lost Button." Next, he colors and cuts out the story event circles. He reads the circles and places them in sequential order, referring to the book as necessary. Then he arranges them in sequential order in a circle on his construction paper square as shown. He glues the circles into place. To finish his project, he draws and colors a picture of his favorite scene from the book in the center of the circle. What a great way to button up sequencing skills!

Pinpointing Perspective

Give your students the opportunity to examine various points of view with a whole-class story retelling! In advance, program an overhead transparency with the book excerpt on this page. Begin by explaining that the story is told by a narrator, which means that the story events are told from an observer's point of view. Further explain that students will be deciding how the story would be different if it were told by Frog or Toad.

Book Excerpt
Toad said, "Frog, you are looking quite green."
"But I always look green," said Frog. "I am a frog."
"Today you look very green even for a frog," said Toad. "Get into my bed and rest."

Rewrite
Toad told me that I was looking quite green. Of course I look green. I am a frog. But he said that I looked greener than I usually do and he told me to get into bed and rest.

Display the transparency on the overhead as a student volunteer reads it aloud. Direct students to imagine that the story is being told by Frog and then have them suggest ways to rewrite the story from his point of view. Write the new story on the transparency.

To extend the lesson, read aloud "A Swim." Have students summarize the story as they work together to retell it from Frog's point of view. Now that's looking at the story in a new light!

Frog and I decided to go swimming. When we got to the river, I...

Snail Mail

Use Toad's experience with his mailbox to inspire your students to brush up on their letter-writing skills *and* examine their ideas about friendship. Begin by reading "The Letter" aloud. Point out that Frog tells Toad that he is his best friend and then ask students to brainstorm a list of the qualities that make up a friend.

Next, review the five parts of a friendly letter. Tell students that they will use the parts of a friendly letter as they write a letter to a classmate. Pair students and direct each child to write a friendly letter to her partner. Encourage her to tell her partner why she thinks he is a good friend. Mount the completed letters on construction paper snail-shaped cutouts and then post them on a board titled "Snail Mail." No doubt these mail-carrying snails will provide a visual reminder of the importance of being a good friend.

date
greeting
body
closing
signature

March 7, 2003
Dear Alex,
   I'm so glad you are my friend. I like to play kickball on your team at recess. Thanks for sharing your snack with me yesterday. You're a great friend!
Your friend,
Elisabeth

Antonym Antics

Leap into an antonym study with events shared by Frog and Toad! In advance, program several sentence strips with sentences such as those listed on this page. For each sentence, program a different index card with the antonym that corresponds with the underlined word.

Begin the activity by writing *wet* and *dry* on the board. Guide students to understand that the words have opposite meanings. Next, display one programmed sentence strip. Ask a student to read aloud the sentence. Then have students choose the card showing the antonym that matches the underlined word. Invite one student to clip the card above its antonym and reread the sentence with the new word. Have another student share how the meaning of the sentence has changed. Continue in this manner as time allows.

Toad is looking <u>sad</u> today.
happy
Frog <u>closes</u> his eyes.
opens
Frog makes <u>small</u> splashes in the water.
big
Every day Toad's mailbox is <u>empty</u>.
full

happy

Toad is looking <u>sad</u> today.

opens

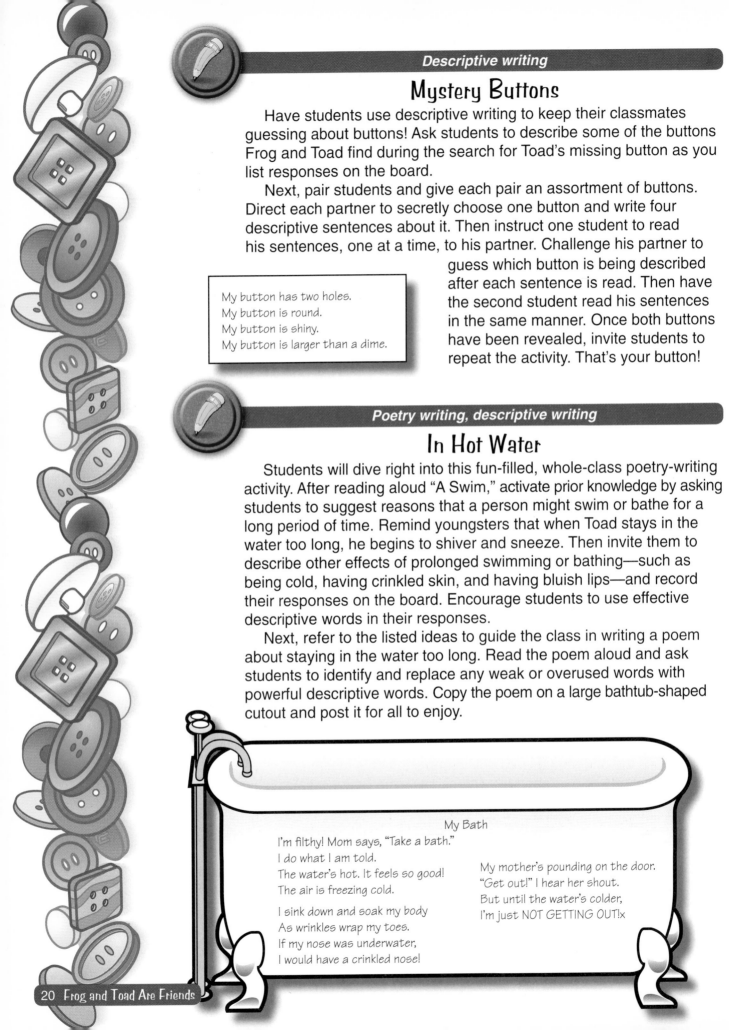

Mystery Buttons

Have students use descriptive writing to keep their classmates guessing about buttons! Ask students to describe some of the buttons Frog and Toad find during the search for Toad's missing button as you list responses on the board.

Next, pair students and give each pair an assortment of buttons. Direct each partner to secretly choose one button and write four descriptive sentences about it. Then instruct one student to read his sentences, one at a time, to his partner. Challenge his partner to guess which button is being described after each sentence is read. Then have the second student read his sentences in the same manner. Once both buttons have been revealed, invite students to repeat the activity. That's your button!

My button has two holes.
My button is round.
My button is shiny.
My button is larger than a dime.

Poetry writing, descriptive writing

In Hot Water

Students will dive right into this fun-filled, whole-class poetry-writing activity. After reading aloud "A Swim," activate prior knowledge by asking students to suggest reasons that a person might swim or bathe for a long period of time. Remind youngsters that when Toad stays in the water too long, he begins to shiver and sneeze. Then invite them to describe other effects of prolonged swimming or bathing—such as being cold, having crinkled skin, and having bluish lips—and record their responses on the board. Encourage students to use effective descriptive words in their responses.

Next, refer to the listed ideas to guide the class in writing a poem about staying in the water too long. Read the poem aloud and ask students to identify and replace any weak or overused words with powerful descriptive words. Copy the poem on a large bathtub-shaped cutout and post it for all to enjoy.

My Bath

I'm filthy! Mom says, "Take a bath."
I do what I am told.
The water's hot. It feels so good!
The air is freezing cold.

I sink down and soak my body
As wrinkles wrap my toes.
If my nose was underwater,
I would have a crinkled nose!

My mother's pounding on the door.
"Get out!" I hear her shout.
But until the water's colder,
I'm just NOT GETTING OUT!x

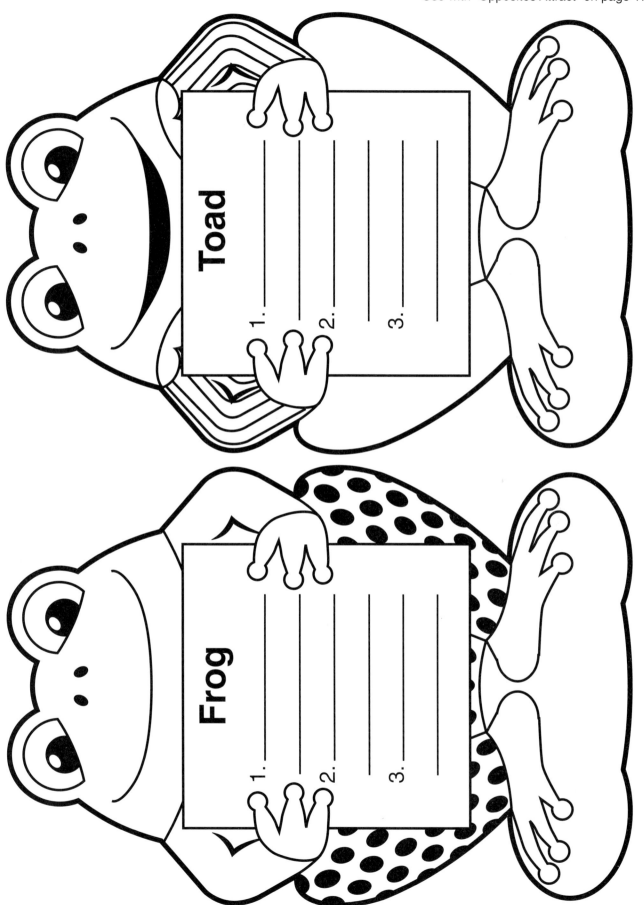

Toad

1.
2.
3.

Frog

1.
2.
3.

Story Event Circles
Use with "Button Lineup" on page 18.

©The Education Center, Inc. • *Reading & Writing With Picture Books* • TEC1791

Tops & Bottoms

Adapted and illustrated by Janet Stevens

In this rustic trickster tale, lazy Bear is the victim of Hare's skillfully planned mischief. In exchange for the use of Bear's land, Hare offers Bear his choice of the next crops: tops or bottoms. Hare plants the garden based on Bear's choice—to Hare's benefit, of course! Time and time again, Hare ends up with the edible parts, whereas Bear gets the useless left-overs. Bear finally wises up to Hare's scheme and decides that he's better off working his own land!

Digging In

Before reading, use this idea to unearth students' agricultural understanding. Begin by inviting youngsters to examine the pictures on the front and back covers of the book. Ask them to share their knowledge about how different vegetables grow, in particular whether the edible parts grow above or below ground. Then invite students to speculate about the title's connection to gardening, leading them to conclude that tops and bottoms refer to the vegetable parts.

Next, read the first two pages of the story. Encourage students to share their predictions about what Hare may be planning, redirecting them to the title if necessary. Continue reading, stopping after the first time Bear realizes that he's been tricked. Ask students to predict what will happen next. Also ask them to make judgments based on questions such as "Do you think Bear should trust Hare again?" and "Does Hare live up to his end of the deal?" Invite students to enjoy the rest of the story, encouraging their predictions and observations as you read.

Planting Order

Help students root out the book's sequence of events with this crafty activity! After reviewing the book, provide each youngster with a copy of the reproducible on page 27, two five-inch green pipe cleaners, and green tissue paper. Have her color the carrot piece patterns, cut them out, and glue them together to assemble the carrot. Next, instruct her to cut out the event cards. Tell her to arrange the events in sequential order on the carrot and then glue each one in place. To make a stem for her carrot, help her tape the pipe cleaner pieces to the top. Have her create leaves by wrapping the tissue paper around the stems and then gluing it in place. Now that's a carrot that's in order from top to bottom!

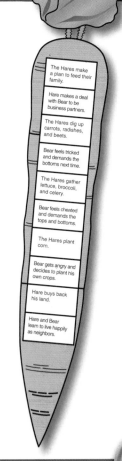

The Hares make a plan to feed their family.

Hare makes a deal with Bear to be business partners.

The Hares dig up carrots, radishes, and beets.

Bear feels tricked and demands the bottoms next time.

The Hares gather lettuce, broccoli, and celery.

Bear feels cheated and demands the tops and bottoms.

The Hares plant corn.

Bear gets angry and decides to plant his own crops.

Hare buys back his land.

Hare and Bear learn to live happily as neighbors.

Character Comparison

This paragraph-writing activity begins with an in-depth look at the characters. Provide each child with a five-inch paper circle and crayons. Have him draw Bear on one side and Hare on the other. Next, read each of the character traits below. As you read each one, have each student decide whether the word describes Bear or Hare throughout most of the story. Then have him display the appropriate side of his circle. Invite a student volunteer to share the reasons behind his choice, using story details to support his answer.

Next, reread the last page of the book to students. Lead students in a discussion of the changes in each character from the beginning of the story to the end. Then give each child a sheet of writing paper. Instruct him to choose either Hare or Bear and write and illustrate a paragraph predicting what may happen next to that character. Bind the completed pages into a class book titled "What's Next for Hare and Bear?" and then place the book in the classroom library.

hardworking	trusting
clever	tricky
wealthy	poor
lazy	angry

Weeding Out Details

This center activity is just "ripe" for helping students recall story details! Display the listed materials at a center. Have each visitor to the center follow the directions to complete his booklet.

Materials:

copy of the book   stapler

construction paper   crayons

half sheets of drawing paper   nonfiction books about vegetables

Directions:

1. Fold one sheet of construction paper in half horizontally.
2. Tuck three half sheets of drawing paper into the folded construction paper and then staple the project to create a booklet.
3. Program the first page "Bear gets the tops and Hare gets the bottoms. Hare plants _____." Complete the sentence by listing the vegetables Hare plants first.
4. In the remaining space, draw the vegetables. If desired, find vegetable pictures in the nonfiction books to refer to as you work.
5. Program the second page "Bear gets the bottoms and Hare gets the tops. Hare plants _____." Complete the sentence and illustrate the page.
6. Program the third page "Bear gets the tops and bottoms. Hare gets the middles. Hare plants _____." Complete the sentence and illustrate the page.
7. Personalize the cover and title the booklet as shown.

Tops, Bottoms, and Middles

Fitch

Bear gets the tops and Hare gets the bottoms. Hare plants carrots, beets, and radishes.

Extra! Extra!

From Hare's perspective, his deals with Bear are smart business. But to Bear, the deals are nothing but tricks! Prompt students' thinking about each character's point of view by leading them in a discussion of the following questions: Why does Hare make the deals? Why does Bear agree to them? What does each character expect to gain? How does Hare feel about the outcome? How does Bear feel about the outcome? Guide students to see the story from each character's point of view.

Next, tell students that they are going to choose one character and write a newspaper article about one of the deals from that character's point of view. Encourage youngsters to consider the following elements: *who* the story is about, *what* took place, *when* and *where* it occurred, and *why* it happened. Then have each child write her article on lined paper. To publish her work, have the child glue her teacher-approved article on a quarter sheet of newsprint and then add a catchy headline. Bind the pages into a class book and invite readers to catch up on the news!

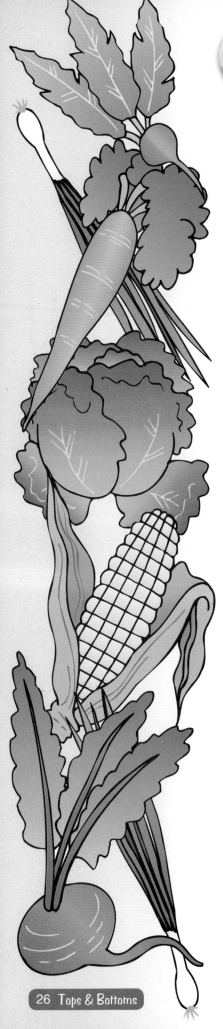

A Crop of Causes and Effects

When it comes to cause and effect, Hare's clever trick provides a harvest of examples! When Bear chooses the tops, Hare plants vegetables with edible bottoms. When Bear demands the bottoms, Hare plants vegetables with edible tops. After sharing these examples with students, invite them to suggest other cause-and-effect relationships from the story. For further practice, have each student complete a copy of page 28.

Cultivating Couplets

Plant the seeds for poetic inspiration with this idea! Begin by pointing out that the two main characters' names (Bear and Hare) rhyme. As a class, brainstorm other story-related rhyming word pairs. List the words on the board. Supplement students' suggestions with the word pairs provided.

Next, explain to students that a *couplet* is two lines of poetry that usually rhyme. Further explain that you will model the writing process for them. To begin, choose a rhyming word pair such as *top* and *crop*. Write the sample couplet on the board. Point out that the rhyming words appear at the end of each line. Then pair students and challenge partners to try their hands at writing their own couplets. If desired, invite interested students to write their polished poetry on vegetable-shaped paper cutouts. Display them on a bulletin board titled "A Fine Crop of Couplets."

sleep—cheap
plan—began
top—crop
beet—cheat
neighbor—labor
grew—chew
weed—greed
deal—steal
trick—pick
fair—hare

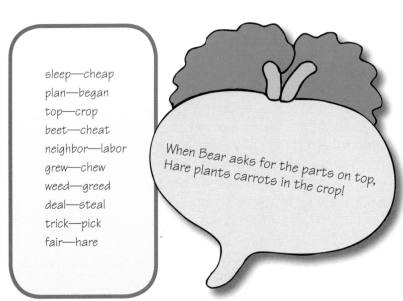

When Bear asks for the parts on top,
Hare plants carrots in the crop!

event cards

The Hares dig up carrots, radishes, and beets.

The Hares gather lettuce, broccoli, and celery.

Bear gets angry and decides to plant his own crops.

The Hares make a plan to feed their family.

Hare and Bear learn to live happily as neighbors.

Bear feels tricked and demands the bottoms next time.

Hare buys back his land.

Bear feels cheated and demands the tops and bottoms.

The Hares plant corn.

Hare makes a deal with Bear to be business partners.

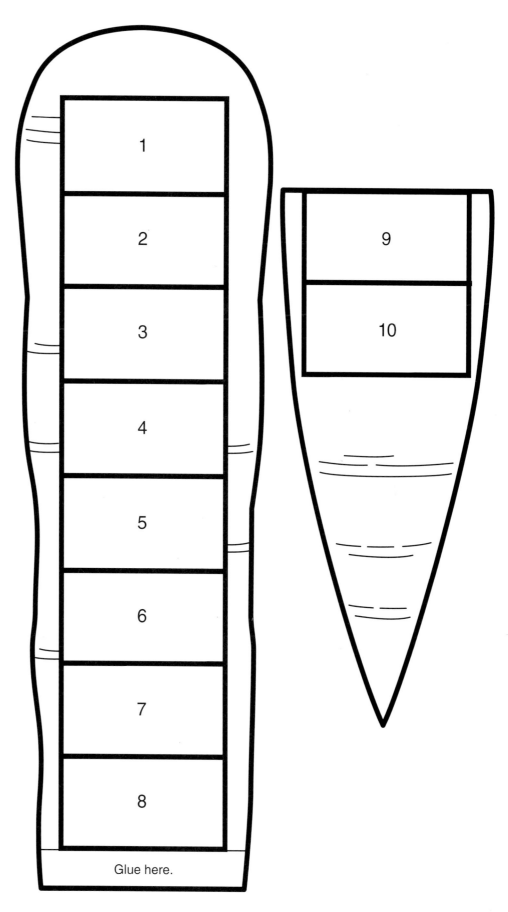

1

2

3

4

5

6

7

8

9

10

Glue here.

Name_____

Matching Crops

Cut out the vegetables at the bottom of the page.
Match each cause sentence with an effect sentence.
Place a dot of glue on each •. Glue each vegetable in place.

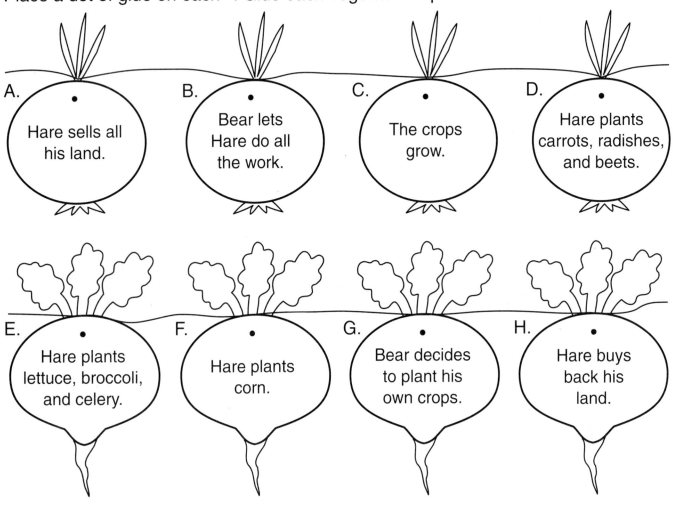

A. Hare sells all his land.

B. Bear lets Hare do all the work.

C. The crops grow.

D. Hare plants carrots, radishes, and beets.

E. Hare plants lettuce, broccoli, and celery.

F. Hare plants corn.

G. Bear decides to plant his own crops.

H. Hare buys back his land.

©The Education Center, Inc. • *Reading & Writing With Picture Books* • TEC1791 • Key p. 80

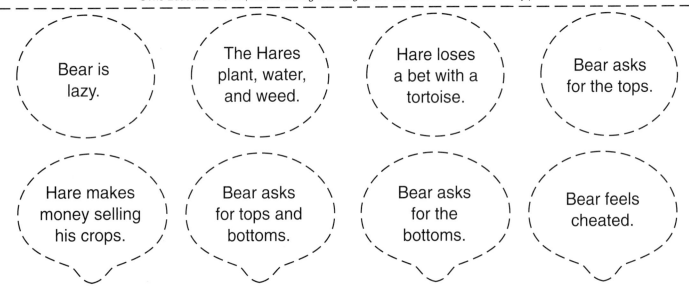

Bear is lazy.

The Hares plant, water, and weed.

Hare loses a bet with a tortoise.

Bear asks for the tops.

Hare makes money selling his crops.

Bear asks for tops and bottoms.

Bear asks for the bottoms.

Bear feels cheated.

Note to the teacher: Use with "A Crop of Causes and Effects" on page 26.

Amazing Grace

Written by Mary Hoffman
Illustrated by Caroline Binch

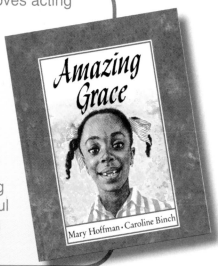

Grace loves stories! She also loves acting out the stories she hears. When her teacher announces that the class is going to perform *Peter Pan,* naturally Grace wants the lead role. Although her classmates discourage her from auditioning for a role that doesn't seem to be a perfect fit, Grace remains determined. Soon she discovers that she can do anything she sets her mind to. This delightful story inspires readers to believe in themselves.

Activating prior knowledge

All About Plays

Before introducing students to Grace, find out what they already know about play auditions and the story of Peter Pan. Begin by leading the class in a discussion of plays. Guide students to understand that plays are live productions and that people play the parts of the characters. Explain that people are chosen to be in plays through an audition process. Have students imagine that they would like to audition for a part in a play. Ask questions such as "What kind of part would you like if you were going to audition for a play?" and "What would you do to prepare for the auditions?" to guide their thinking.

Next, explain to students that they will be studying a book about a girl who loves to act out stories. Further explain that the girl's class will be doing the play *Peter Pan.* Ask students to think about Peter Pan. Have them brainstorm words that describe him, and list their ideas on the board. Then gather students in a circle and read aloud *Amazing Grace.* Pause at appropriate points to allow students to predict what will happen next. Students will be surprised and delighted to learn that Grace, who may not fit their listed descriptions, makes the perfect Peter Pan!

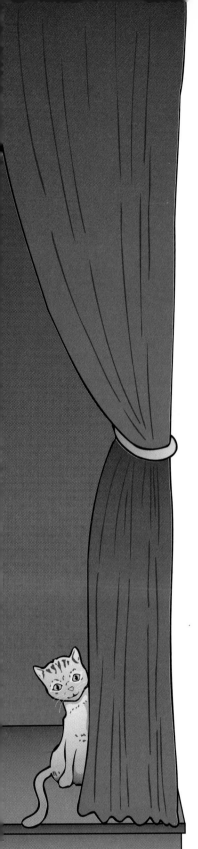

An Amazing Story!

This thought-provoking activity provides sentence-writing practice. Reread the book aloud, stopping after Nana tells Grace, "You can be anything you want, Grace, if you put your mind to it." Ask each student to imagine what he would do if he was in Grace's place; would he still be determined to audition for the part of Peter Pan? Provide time for students to consider this question.

Next, continue reading, stopping after Natalie whispers, "You were fantastic!" Ask each student to think about how he would vote if he were in Grace's class; would he have voted for Grace too? Allow time for students to think about their opinions and then finish rereading the book. To give each child an opportunity to record his thoughts, give him a copy of page 33. Encourage the child to write his responses in complete sentences.

Deciphering Details

Story details will come together after students complete this sorting center. In advance, gather two sentence strips, scissors, and a marker. Program one sentence strip with the true statements on this page. Write the statements so that they are spaced equally apart on the strip as shown. Next, cut different jagged lines between each pair of statements and then set the pieces aside. Repeat the steps with the second sentence strip and the false statements. Shuffle both sets of pieces together and then display them, along with a copy of *Amazing Grace,* at a center.

Direct each child to read each statement. As he reads, have him sort the pieces into piles of true and false statements. To check his work, have him arrange the pieces into the original strip shapes. Now that's an activity that sets the story straight!

True

| Grace acts out many different stories. | Nana takes Grace to the ballet. | Nana and Ma sometimes help Grace act out her stories. | Grace uses her stuffed animals to help her act out the roles. | Grace's friends don't think she should play Peter Pan. | Grace plays Peter Pan in the play. |

False

| Nana takes Grace to the movies. | Grace lives with her pa and ma. | Grace likes to act out mystery stories the best. | Grace plays the part of Tinkerbell in the play. | Ma eats lunch with Grace in the park. | Grace wants to become a doctor when she grows up. |

Uncovering Character Traits

Amazing is certainly a word that describes Grace! Have your students complete this activity to find other words that describe her. After sharing the book aloud, have students brainstorm words that describe Grace, and list their suggestions on the board. Encourage students to give examples from the book to support each description. Next, provide a copy of page 34 for each child. Have her choose four words from the brainstormed list. Then have her complete the page as directed.

Starring Facts and Opinions

Grace is the star of the play! Your students will be stars at distinguishing fact from opinion after they complete this colorful mobile. Remind students that a *fact* can be proven to be true, whereas an *opinion* may not be true in every case. Read the following sentences aloud: "Grace likes to act out different stories" and "She plays exciting characters." Have students decide which sentence is a fact and which is an opinion. Invite students to give other examples of fact and opinion statements from the story.

Next, provide each student with the listed materials and guide him through the steps below to complete his mobile.

Materials for each student:
sheet each of black, yellow,
   and orange construction paper
access to a star-shaped template
scissors
yarn
glue
white crayon
pencil
ruler
access to a hole puncher

Steps:
1. Fold the black paper in half lengthwise. Keeping the fold at the top use the white crayon to write "Starring Facts and Opinions" on each side. Then draw several stars on each side.
2. Use the template, the remaining construction paper, and scissors to make four orange stars and four yellow stars.
3. Write a fact from the story on each orange star and an opinion on each yellow star.
4. Cut four eight-inch yarn lengths.
5. Glue like-colored stars back to back so that one end of a different yarn length is sandwiched in between each pair.
6. Glue the opposite end of each yarn length in between the black paper so that the stars are hanging at various lengths as shown.
7. Punch two holes on either end of the folded side of the black paper. Cut a 24-inch yarn length. Tie each end of the yarn through one of the holes.

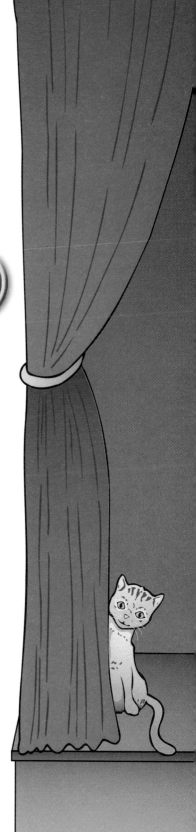

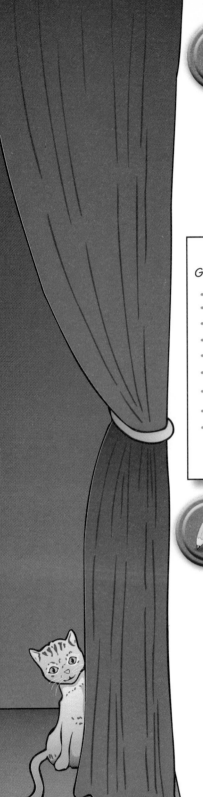

Spotlight on Grace

Use this article-writing activity to highlight Grace and her accomplishments! Explain to students that the message of the book is also called the *theme*. Further explain that other literary elements such as *characters* and *plot* help to develop the theme. To focus students' thinking, lead them in a discussion of the following questions: Who is the main character? What conflicts does the character face? How are the conflicts resolved? What does the character learn through the events in the story? Then ask students to decide what the theme of *Amazing Grace* is. Lead students to understand that despite discouragement from her peers, Grace follows her dream.

Next, have each student imagine that she is a newspaper reporter. Direct her to imagine that she has interviewed Grace and some of her family and friends. Have the child write a feature article about Grace. Encourage her to include Grace's struggles as well as her accomplishments in the article. Instruct the child to write a headline for her completed article. Bind the articles into a book titled "Grace in the News."

Despite What Others Think, Grace Keeps Her Goal in Sight!

Great Goals

Grace is determined to get the lead role in the school play. But it's not just her determination that lands her the part! Ask students to name some of the many factors that help Grace accomplish her goal (*seeks support from the adults in her life, acts out stories, and practices for the audition*).

Next, give each child a sheet of white construction paper and have him fold his paper into six equal sections as shown. Instruct him to think of a goal—big or small— that he would like to accomplish in the future. In the first section, direct him to write a sentence describing his goal. Then, in each of the remaining sections, have him write a sentence describing one of the steps he could take to bring him closer to meeting his goal. Finally, direct the child to illustrate each sentence. Provide time for each student to share his work with the class.

I want to become a vet.	I can help my dad with the farm animals.	 I can ask my mom if I can have a pet to take care of.
Later I could work with a vet and watch what he does.	I can go to high school and study hard.	 Finally, I will go to vet school.

An Amazing Story!

Think about the story.
Answer each question. Write your answer in complete sentences.

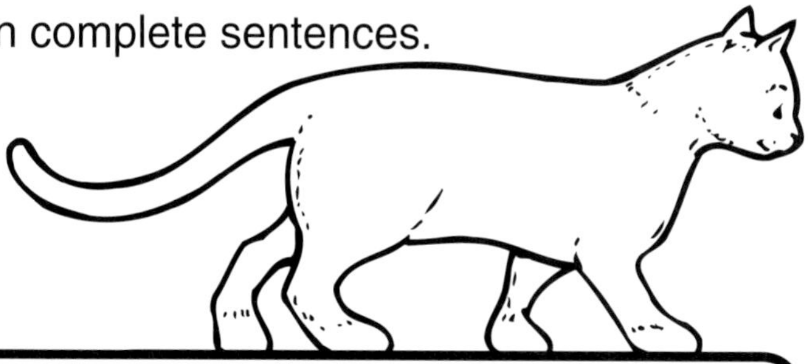

1. Even though her friends tell her she can't, Grace auditions for the part of Peter Pan. If you were Grace, what would you do?

_____

_____

_____

_____

2. Do you think Grace should have the part? Why or why not?

_____

_____

_____

_____

3. Would you want to have a person like Grace for a friend? Why or why not?

_____

_____

_____

_____

Note to the teacher: Use with "An Amazing Story!" on page 30.

Uncovering Character Traits

Complete each book title by writing one word that describes Grace.
Below each title, write sentences to explain how the title describes Grace.

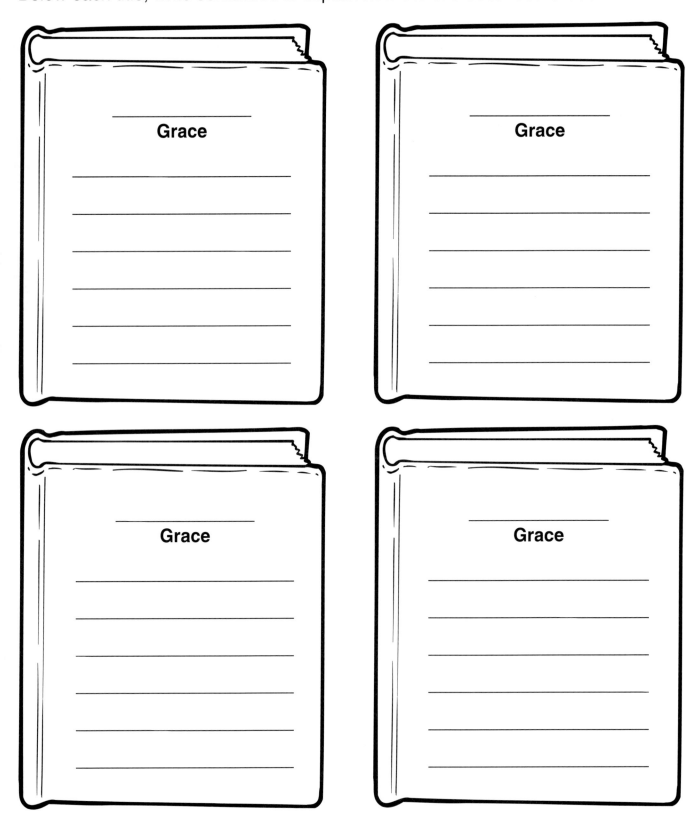

Sheila Rae, the Brave

Written and illustrated by Kevin Henkes

Sheila Rae walks backward with her eyes closed, steps on cracks, and even growls at stray dogs. In fact, Sheila Rae is not afraid of anything! That is, until one day when she takes a wrong turn on her way home from school and becomes very scared. Luckily, her little sister comes to the rescue, showing young readers what bravery and sibling love are all about!

Setting

Setting the Scene

Simplify the concept of setting by having students create these picture projects! Remind students that to find the setting, they must find the story's location and the time in which it takes place. Further explain that story pictures and events can give the reader clues about the setting. Then gather students around you and show them each two-page spread in *Sheila Rae, the Brave*. Guide students in a discussion of where and when each event takes place. To focus students' thinking, pose questions such as the following: Does the story take place in the suburbs or in the city? What time of year is it? How do you know?

Next, give each child a sheet of drawing paper and instruct her to illustrate and color one of the story settings. For example, the child may draw a house, a field, or a neighborhood. On the back of her paper, have the child write sentences explaining how she knows that this is one of the story's settings. Provide time for each child to share her work with the class.

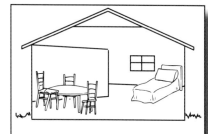

Part of the story happens in a house. I know because there's a bed in one picture and a dining room table in another.

Branching Out

For a leafy paragraph-writing lesson, start with this terrific tree activity! After reviewing *Sheila Rae, the Brave*, tell students that the main idea of a story is its theme. Lead students in a discussion of the book, guiding them to conclude that the main idea is that everyone can be brave sometimes and scared sometimes.

Next, give one copy of the tree pattern on page 39 to each child. Instruct the child to copy the main idea on the tree's trunk. Then ask students to recall story details that support the main idea. Encourage them to consider details from the text as well as details from the pictures. Ask questions such as the following: What does Sheila Rae do that tells you she's brave? When is Sheila Rae afraid? Who is brave when Sheila Rae is afraid? Then direct the student to write one detail on each tree branch.

To complete the activity, explain to each student that the main idea he's listed can be used as a topic sentence for a paragraph. Give the child a sheet of writing paper and have him refer to his tree page as he writes a paragraph explaining the story's theme.

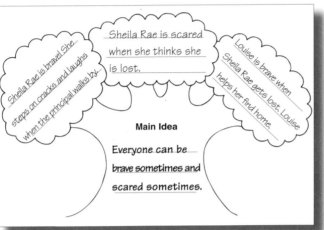

Sheila Rae is brave. She steps on cracks and laughs when the principal walks by.

Sheila Rae is scared when she thinks she is lost.

Louise is brave when Sheila Rae gets lost. Louise helps her find home.

Main Idea

Everyone can be brave sometimes and scared sometimes.

Character Comparisons

No doubt your students will find many things to like about Sheila Rae, but how much do they have in common with her? These character glyphs help students explore this question. Give one copy of page 40 to each child and then provide time for her to complete the glyph.

As each student finishes her page, have her trim the picture as shown and then set it aside. Give her a sheet of writing paper and have her write a short paragraph explaining how she is like Sheila Rae, not like her, or like her in some ways and different in others. To create a colorful character display, have the child trim her paragraph and then mount it, along with her glyph picture, on construction paper. Staple the projects onto a bulletin board titled "Sheila Rae and Me."

Puzzling Through the Details

This reading center is sure to build students' story recall skills! In advance, program eight sentence strips, each with one of the phrases listed on this page. Next, cut a different jagged line between each beginning verb and the rest of the phrase, as shown, and then store the pieces at a center. In addition, place a copy of the book, a supply of writing paper, and pencils in the center.

Instruct each student to read the pieces and then match them to form phrases that describe story events. Once the child has finished matching the phrases, have him write eight sentences on a sheet of writing paper. For each sentence, tell him to use a different phrase from his puzzle pieces. Encourage him to add extra words as needed and to use proper punctuation and capitalization.

steps on every crack
rides her bicycle
walks backward with her eyes closed
growls at stray dogs
turns corners
crosses streets
pretends that the trees are evil creatures
hugs her sister

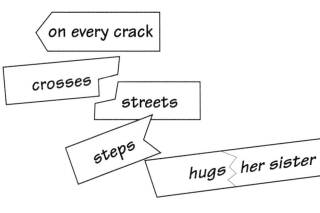

on every crack

crosses

streets

steps

hugs her sister

Fearless Charades

Use this fun activity to inspire students to recall the story details that prove Sheila Rae's bravery! Begin by having students brainstorm examples of Sheila Rae's brave actions, such as giggling when the principal walks by or walking backward with her eyes closed. List each suggestion on a separate index card and then place the cards in a basket.

Next, divide students into small groups. Invite one member from each group to draw a card and then share it with his group. Then direct each group, in turn, to act out the assigned action while the other groups guess what is being depicted.

Neighborhood Nouns

Sheila Rae is likely to pop up all over the place during this proper-noun-writing practice! In advance, make several construction paper street signs and post them around the classroom. Use a strip of gray paper to make a pole for each sign.

To begin, have student volunteers suggest local street names as you write each one on a separate sign. Point out that each word in the street's name is capitalized. Explain to students that they will use the street names in sentences they write about Sheila Rae. Next, give one sheet of writing paper to each child and direct him to write ten sentences, being careful to capitalize Sheila Rae's name and the street's name. To publish his work, instruct the child to choose one sentence to copy on the top of a 6" x 9" white construction paper rectangle. In the remaining space, invite him to illustrate his sentence. Then have him use a loop of tape to post his sentence near the corresponding street sign.

Galvin Road

Sheila Rae growls at dogs on Galvin Road.

Fearless Feats

This creative-writing activity will have students imagining just how fearless Sheila Rae can be! Remind students that Sheila Rae brags about being fearless in many different situations—but all in familiar surroundings. To inspire students to explore Sheila Rae's fearlessness in other settings, have them brainstorm places she could visit as you list each suggestion on the board.

Next, direct each child to choose one setting from the list on the board. Have her write a list of things Sheila Rae might encounter in her chosen setting. Then instruct her to refer to her list as she writes a sequel to *Sheila Rae, the Brave.* Bind the completed stories into a book titled "Fearless Sheila Rae," and place the book in the classroom library. There's no telling what fearless feats Sheila Rae will attempt next!

Rain Forest
big bugs
giant snakes
towering trees

Settings
Hospital
Rain Forest
City

Sheila Rae wasn't afraid of anything. When her class visited the rain forest, she invited the big bugs to join her for tea. She proudly wore a giant snake like a necklace. She even climbed towering trees to get a better view!

Name _____

Main Idea

_____
_____
_____

©The Education Center, Inc. • *Reading & Writing With Picture Books* • TEC1791

Note to the teacher: Use with "Branching Out" on page 36.

39

Name _____

40

Alike or Different?

Choose the answer that tells about you.
Add the matching decoration to the mouse picture.

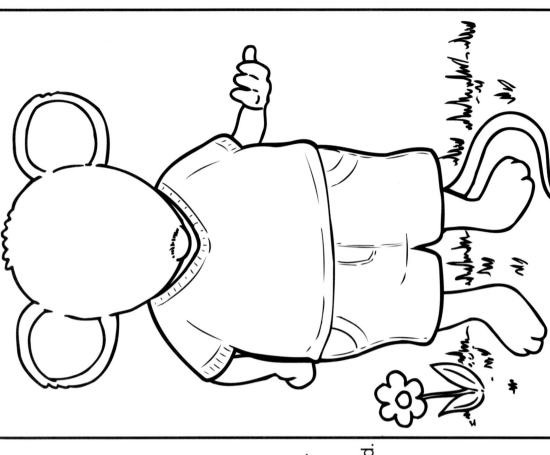

1. Sheila Rae is a girl.
   I'm a girl too. = Color the shirt and shorts red.
   I'm a boy. = Color the shirt and shorts blue.

2. Sheila Rae has one sister.
   I have one sister too. = Draw four whiskers.
   I have no sisters or more than one. = Draw six whiskers.

3. Sheila Rae rides a bike.
   I can ride a bike too. = Draw two open eyes.
   I don't know how to ride a bike yet. = Draw two closed eyes.

4. Sheila Rae steps on cracks on the sidewalk.
   I step on cracks too. = Draw a lunchbox in the mouse's hand.
   I don't step on cracks. = Draw a ball in the mouse's hand.

5. Sheila Rae is frightened when she loses her way.
   I feel frightened sometimes too. = Color the fur brown.
   I never feel frightened. = Color the fur black.

6. Color the rest of your picture.

Note to the teacher: Use with "Character Comparisons" on page 36.

Today Was a Terrible Day

Written by Patricia Reilly Giff
Illustrated by Susanna Natti

After a school day filled with calamities, poor Ronald Morgan doesn't think he can do anything right! Luckily for Ronald—and young readers alike—he finds a reason to smile when he discovers what a truly compassionate person he has for a teacher!

Could It Be Worse?

Before sharing the book, inspire students to speculate about story events with this group activity! In advance, program five sheets of chart paper, each with a different school setting from the story (see samples). Explain to students that they'll be listening to a story about a boy's bad day at school. Display the book's cover and have students brainstorm events or situations that could make a school day bad.

Next, divide students into small groups and provide each group with one of the preprogrammed sheets and crayons. Have the group list things that could go wrong in the assigned setting as shown. After a select amount of time, invite one group member to share her group's ideas, and post the charts in a visible location.

Gather students around and read the book aloud. Guide students to compare their predictions with the actual events. They may soon see that Ronald's day could have been even worse!

classroom

water fountain

lunchroom

hallway

playground

fall and skin your knees
get in an argument with a friend
kick the ball over the fence
have to sit in time-out

Story-Element Pass

Here's a catching game that reinforces story elements! After reading the book aloud, ask students to sit in a circle on the floor. Gently toss a beanbag to one child as you call out one of the following story elements: character, setting, or event (plot). Instruct the child to name an example from the book that matches the element and then gently toss the beanbag back to you. Continue in this manner until each child has had a turn. For more story-element practice, have each child complete a copy of page 45.

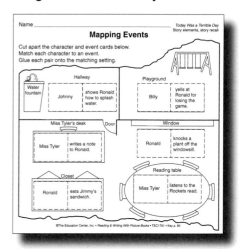

What's Next?

Use these flip booklets to help students identify cause and effect. After sharing the book with students, lead a discussion about how many of Ronald's actions lead to a consequence that increases the troubles of his terrible day. List several of the effect-producing actions on the board (see the list on this page). Next, give each student a sheet of 12" x 18" white construction paper. Guide the child through the directions below to make his flip book.

> Ronald drops his pencil.
> Ronald's stomach starts growling.
> Ronald doesn't know how to do the workbook page.
> Ronald puts his finger over the faucet.
> Ronald misses the ball.
> Ronald waters the plants.

Directions:
1. Fold the construction paper in half horizontally.
2. With the fold at the top, fold the paper in half vertically two times.
3. Open the last two folds. Cut the top layer on the three fold lines to make four flaps as shown.
4. Copy and illustrate a different action from the list on each flap.
5. Write and illustrate the effect of each action under the corresponding flap.

Character Conversations

The conversations in *Today Was a Terrible Day* provide the perfect springboard for a dialogue-writing lesson. Ask students to brainstorm words that signal that a character is speaking—such as *said, yelled,* and *asked*—and list their ideas on the board. Next, reread the book aloud. Direct students to listen for the listed words and raise their hands each time a dialogue example is read. After reading, write several dialogue examples on the board, omitting the quotation marks. Invite volunteers to write in the missing punctuation marks. For individual dialogue practice, have each child complete a copy of page 46. Characters can sure have a way with words!

asked
yelled
said

A Dynamite Day

Turn Ronald's day from terrible to terrific with this collaborative class book! To begin, have students recall events from Ronald's day as you list each one on the board. Next, pair students and assign one event from the list to each pair. Direct the partners to brainstorm ways that something good instead of bad could have happened in their assigned situation. For example, instead of spraying water on Joy at the fountain, Ronald could have behaved quietly and received praise from Mrs. Gallop. Then instruct each pair to choose one of its ideas and write a paragraph describing the good things that happened to Ronald. Have the partners trim around their paragraph and then glue it onto a sheet of drawing paper. Finally, encourage the pair to use crayons to decorate the paper. Once each pair has finished, have the class work together to write an ending for Ronald's fabulous day. Bind all of the pages into a book titled "Today Was a Terrific Day" and then read the book aloud. Now, that's a great day!

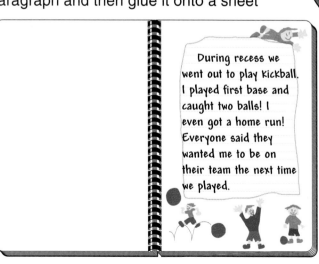

During recess we went out to play kickball. I played first base and caught two balls! I even got a home run! Everyone said they wanted me to be on their team the next time we played.

A Note for the Teacher

Students are sure to recognize the importance of encouraging words after completing this letter-writing activity! Begin by rereading Miss Tyler's note to Ronald. Guide students in a discussion of why she would write such a nice note, considering the kind of day Ronald had. Have them recall Ronald's feelings after reading the note *(happy, plans to give Miss Tyler a plant).* Lead students to conclude that encouraging words can cheer someone up after a disappointing day.

Next, give each student a sheet of writing paper. Direct the student to imagine that he is Ronald. Then have him write a letter to give Miss Tyler along with the plant. Remind the child to include the five parts of a friendly letter (date, greeting, body, closing, and signature). Provide time for each child to read his completed letter aloud. What a pleasant way to improve letter-writing skills *and* encourage kindness!

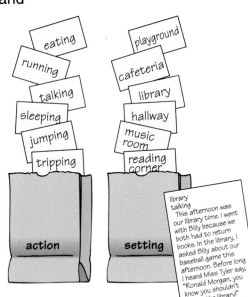

October 4, 2005

Dear Miss Tyler,
Thank you for your nice note. It made me smile even though I was having a bad day. I'm really sorry that I broke your plant. I hope you like the new one even if it's not the same.

Love,
Ronald

Snakey's Situations

This scenario-setting center is sure to get your students' creative juices flowing! In advance, program two paper bags and two sets of index cards as shown. Put each set of cards into its corresponding bag and place the bags at a center stocked with paper and pencils.

At the center, a student selects one card from each bag to create a new situation for Ronald. She writes the words at the top of her paper. Next, she imagines that she is Ronald and writes a story to correspond with the selected scenario. Once she's finished, the student illustrates her story as time allows.

eating
running
talking
sleeping
jumping
tripping

playground
cafeteria
library
hallway
music room
reading corner

action

setting

library
talking
This afternoon was our library time. I went with Billy because we both had to return books. In the library, I asked Billy about our baseball game this afternoon. Before long, I heard Miss Tyler say, "Ronald Morgan, you know you shouldn't talk in the library!"

Mapping Events

Cut apart the character and event cards below.
Match each character to an event.
Glue each pair onto the matching setting.

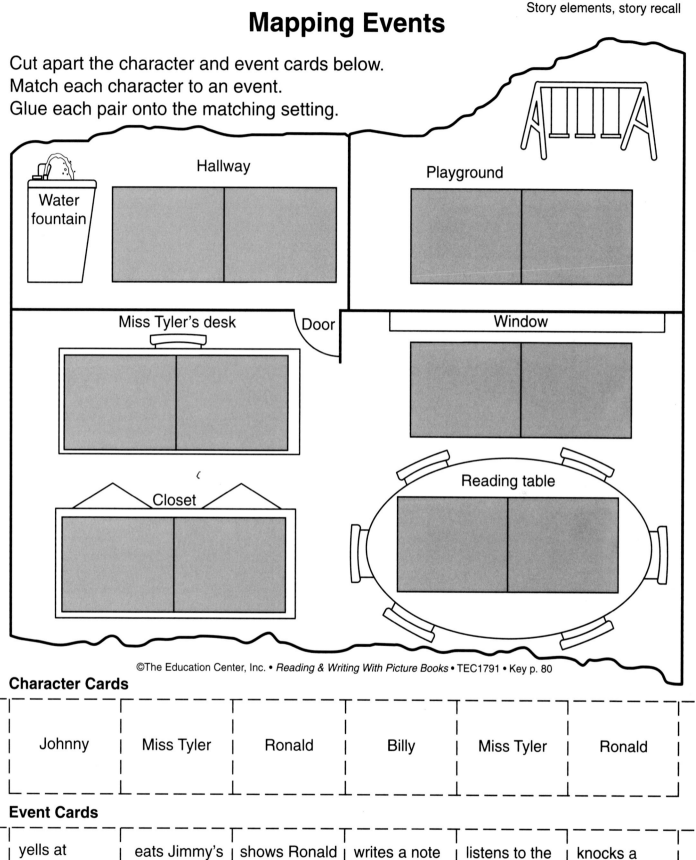

©The Education Center, Inc. • *Reading & Writing With Picture Books* • TEC1791 • Key p. 80

Character Cards

| Johnny | Miss Tyler | Ronald | Billy | Miss Tyler | Ronald |

Event Cards

| yells at Ronald for losing the game. | eats Jimmy's sandwich. | shows Ronald how to splash water. | writes a note to Ronald. | listens to the Rockets read. | knocks a plant off the windowsill. |

Note to the teacher: Use with "Story-Element Pass" on page 42.

Desktop Dialogue

Read each sentence.
Decide whether Ronald or Miss Tyler is the speaker.
Fill in the blank with the character's name.
Add quotation marks to show the speaker's exact words.

1.
Why do you look
like a snake under
that table?
asked _____.

2.
_____ asked,
Why are you eating
Jimmy's sandwich in
the closet?

3.
I forgot to have my
mother sign my
homework,
said _____.

4.
_____ asked,
Can you help me with
my workbook page?

5.
I hope I get to go to
third grade, said
_____.

6.
You need to look
at that word again,
said _____.

7.
_____ said,
I knocked the
plant off the
windowsill.

8.
I wish I could read as
well as Billy, thought
_____.

9.
_____ said,
I think you can
read this note by
yourself.

Bonus Box: What do you think Miss Tyler will say when Ronald gives her the plant? Use quotation marks to write your answer.

Alexander and the Wind-Up Mouse

Written and illustrated by Leo Lionni

Alexander the mouse longs for love and attention, but is met instead with screams and a broom. When he meets Willy, a well-loved toy mouse, he becomes even more dissatisfied with his lonely life. Alexander approaches a magical garden lizard who agrees to grant his wish to become a toy mouse. But when Alexander learns that Willy has been replaced by new toys, his plans change. In the end, Willy becomes a real mouse and Alexander's wish for friendship is granted.

Main idea and supporting details

Sweeping Up the Main Idea

When it comes to finding main idea and supporting details, this broom-making activity really cleans up! As you read the book aloud, challenge students to listen for the main idea, or the most important idea of the story. After reading, guide students to identify one possible main idea—that Alexander is lonely. Write it on the chalkboard. Then have students brainstorm story details that support the main idea.

Next, provide each student with a three-inch red construction paper square and four 1½" x 8" strips of brown paper. To make her broom, the child glues three strips to the red square as shown. She trims the square and then signs her name. She glues the remaining strip at the top to form the broom handle. Then she copies the main idea on the broom handle and writes a supporting detail on each of the bristles. Display students' completed projects on a bulletin board with a mouse cutout. Title the board "Cleaning Up With Supporting Details."

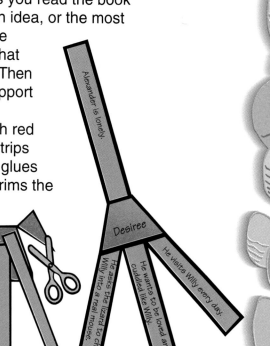

Turning Words Into Sentences

This mousy writing center increases students' vocabulary skills! Enlarge the mouse pattern on this page and then make enough construction paper copies for each child to have two. Next, make five pebble-shaped cutouts from purple construction paper. Program each pebble with one of the vocabulary words shown below. Display the pebbles and mouse patterns at the center along with a dictionary, a copy of *Alexander and the Wind-Up Mouse,* scissors, and pencils.

Instruct each child who vists the center to read each pebble word. Next, have him find the word in the book and read the page on which the word is found. If he is unsure of its meaning after reading the word in context, invite him to look up the word in the dictionary. Finally, on each of his mouse cutouts, have him write a sentence that includes at least one pebble word. Display the cutouts on a bulletin board titled "Alexander and the Vocabulary Mice."

ordinary
adventures
mysteriously
precious
alas

©The Education Center, Inc. • *Reading & Writing With Picture Books* • TEC1791

Can You Believe It?

Open students' eyes to factual and fictional story events with this activity. After rereading the book aloud, prompt students to discuss the differences between Alexander and Willy. Lead them to conclude that Alexander is a real mouse, and Willy is a toy. Point out that in a similar way, the story has events that could really happen, as well as events that are only make-believe.

To practice distinguishing between real and make-believe story events, give two index cards to each student. Have her draw a real mouse on one card and a wind-up mouse on the other card. Then gather students for another reading of the story. At appropriate points, ask each child to hold up the card that indicates whether the passage could or couldn't really happen. Scan students' cards to check for accuracy. For further practice, have each child complete a copy of page 51.

Tossing Out Ideas

At first, Alexander envies Willy's life and wants to be just like him. But by the end of the story, Alexander learns that he's better off the way he is. Draw upon this lesson to spark a meaningful dialogue with your students. Gather students in a circle. Use the questions shown to guide a literary discussion. To encourage participation, gently toss a purple beanbag to a student who is ready to respond to a question. When she is finished, have her toss the beanbag back to you. Continue as time allows. The lesson of this mouse tale? Trying to be someone else isn't always best!

> When he is alone, Alexander thinks of Willy with envy. Why does Alexander want to be like his friend?
>
> Have you ever wanted to be like someone else? Who? Explain why.
>
> Alexander asks the lizard to turn him into Willy. Do you think this is the right thing to do?
>
> Before Alexander finds the purple pebble, he learns that Willy is going to be thrown away. How might the story be different if Alexander found a purple pebble right away?
>
> All along Alexander thinks Willy has the better life. What does he learn in the end?
>
> What can you learn from this story about who you are?

Pleasingly Persuasive

Here's the perfect activity to prompt students' power to persuade! Revisit the part of the story when Alexander learns that Willy is to be thrown away. Discuss with students any experience they've had throwing away old toys or trying to talk their parents out of doing so.

Next, have youngsters brainstorm other possibilities for the toys, such as selling them at a yard sale or donating them to charity. List their ideas on the board. Then guide each child in writing a persuasive letter to Annie from Alexander. Encourage him to include at least three alternatives for Willy and reasons why those options would be better than throwing him away. Invite students to share their completed letters with the class.

> Dear Annie,
>
> I am writing to persuade you not to throw Willy away. You could sell him at a yard sale and make some money for yourself. You could donate him to charity so that some other child could play with him. The best idea is to give him to me. Then Willy and I could still be friends. I hope that you do not throw him away.
>
> Sincerely,
> Alexander

Purple Pebble Prompts

Narrative-writing practice is just a stone's throw away with this idea! Program four lizard-shaped cutouts, each with a different prompt from below. Mount the cutouts onto a bulletin board as shown. Next, trim a class supply of writing paper into large pebble shapes. Display the pebble-shaped writing paper and purple construction paper near the bulletin board.

During free time, encourage students to visit the board. Have each child choose a prompt and write her response on a sheet of prepared writing paper. Next, tell her to glue her writing onto a purple sheet of construction paper and then trim around the shape, leaving a half-inch border. Mount her completed project below the appropriate lizard.

- If you were the lizard, what payment would you ask for instead of the purple pebble? Tell why.
- How might the story ending be different if Alexander found a purple pebble right away?
- What do you think happened to the purple pebble?
- If you could change into someone else for one day, who would it be? Why?

Squeaking Out Poetry

With your guidance, students will be scurrying to compose poetry! Before beginning, give a copy of page 52 to each child. On a sheet of chart paper, prepare six rows and number them 1–6 as shown. Write "Alexander" in the first row. In each remaining row, list student-suggested words or phrases according to the directions on page 52.

Next, instruct each student to choose Willy or Alexander to feature in his own poem. Have him write his poem on his copy of page 52. Provide time for students to share their completed poems with the class.

1.	Alexander
2.	lonely, sad
3.	chased by brooms
4.	meets a friend
5.	happy, excited
6.	real

Can You Believe It?

Read each sentence.
Color Alexander if the event could really happen.
Color Willy if the event is make-believe.

	Real	Make-Believe
1. Every time they see Alexander they chase him with a broom.		
2. Alexander hears a squeak in Annie's room.		
3. "Who are you?" asks Alexander.		
4. Alexander and Willy become friends.		
5. One day Willy tells a strange story about a magic lizard.		
6. The lizard tells Alexander to bring him a purple pebble.		
7. Annie is going to throw Willy away.		
8. Alexander sees a purple pebble.		
9. There is a full moon.		
10. The lizard changes Willy into a real mouse.		
11. Alexander runs back to the house as fast as he can.		
12. Alexander and Willy dance until dawn.		

Bonus Box: Choose a make-believe sentence from above. On the back of this sheet, explain why it could not happen in real life.

Mousy Poetry

Line 1 Choose a mouse from *Alexander and the Wind-Up Mouse.* Write his name.

Line 2 Write two words that tell how the mouse feels at the beginning of the story.

Line 3 Write three words that tell why he feels that way.

Line 4 Write three words that tell why his feelings change.

Line 5 Write two words that describe his new feelings.

Line 6 Write a word that describes the mouse.

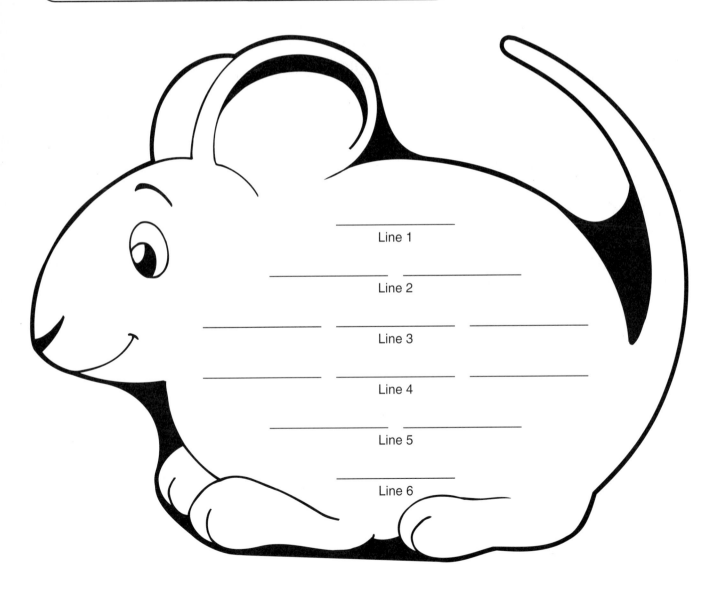

Line 1

Line 2

Line 3

Line 4

Line 5

Line 6

Flossie & the Fox

Written by Patricia C. McKissack
Illustrated by Rachel Isadora

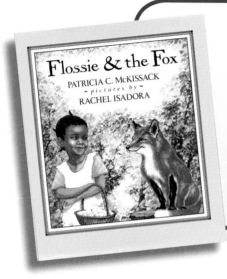

The neighbor's hens have been so terrorized by a fox that they have stopped laying eggs. So Flossie takes a basket of eggs to the neighbor's house. Along the way, she encounters the infamous fox. Flossie, showing no fear, challenges him to prove he's a fox. A humorous battle of wills and wits begins, eventually resulting in an "outfoxing" by Flossie.

Activating prior knowledge

Finding Out About Foxes

Use this prereading research activity to get your students thinking about foxes. In advance, gather several nonfiction books about foxes. Explain to students that they will soon be listening to a tale about a fox and a little girl. Then ask them what they already know about foxes and list their responses on the board.

Next, divide students into small groups. Provide each group with a copy of page 57. Instruct the group to complete the page as directed, referring to the nonfiction books as they need to. Once the pages are complete, provide time for students to share their findings. Aren't foxes fascinating?

Comparing Conflicts

Looking for a literature-based lesson on conflict and resolution? Try this whole-class activity! To prepare, create a chart with two rows and three columns labeled at the top as shown. Begin by asking students to recall the two main characters from the book as you write them in the first column. Invite volunteers to describe each character's problem; list their descriptions in the second column of the appropriate row.

Next, direct students to listen for each character's problem-solving actions as you reread the book aloud. Each time a student hears an action, have him raise his hand and point it out to the class. List each action in the third column of the appropriate row. Before you resume reading, lead students in a discussion of the character's progress in solving his problem. By the end of the book, students are sure to see that although the problem may not work out exactly the way the character intends it to, each character's problem is solved!

Character	Problem	Solution
Flossie	Flossie needs to take the eggs to the McCutchin place.	She takes a shorter route through the woods. She stops the fox from taking the eggs by telling him she thinks he is a rabbit. She tells the fox she thinks he is a rat.
Fox	Fox wants to convince Flossie that he's really a fox.	He tells Flossie that he has soft fur. He tells Flossie that he has a pointed nose. He asks the cat to tell Flossie that he is who he says he is.

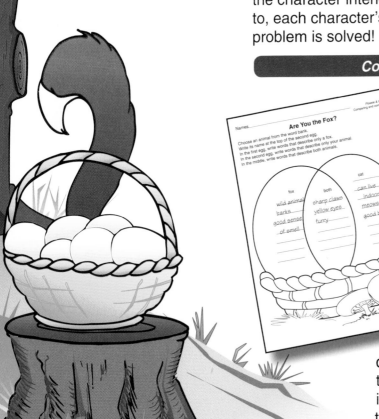

Creature Comparisons

Flossie certainly thinks that the fox has a lot in common with other animals. At this research center, students learn for themselves what features a fox shares with other animals. Stock the center with pencils, a supply of copies of page 58, a copy of *Flossie & the Fox,* and nonfiction books about the animals listed on page 58.

Instruct each student pair to complete page 58 as directed. Encourage them to refer to the books to learn information about its chosen animal. Have the pair write the information on the page. Once the comparisons are complete, your students can decide for themselves whether or not a fox is unique!

Dialect Dictionary

Use this class dictionary to launch your students into a study of *Flossie and the fox's* vocabulary! In advance, program a set of index cards, each with a different sentence from the list on this page. Pair students and distribute a different card to each pair. Next, instruct each pair to listen for its sentence as you reread the book aloud. Pause after a pair's sentence is read, reread the passage surrounding the sentence, and invite the pair to use context clues to interpret the sentence's meaning aloud.

Next, give each pair a sheet of white paper. Direct the partners to copy their sentence across the top of the paper. Then have them write their interpretation of the sentence at the bottom of the page. Finally, direct the pair to draw and color an illustration in the remaining space. Once all pages are complete, bind them into a booklet titled "Flossie and the Fox's Vocabulary." Display the book in the class library for students to enjoy.

"Seem like they been troubled by a fox."
"Ever-time they corner that ol' slickster, he gets away."
"I disremember ever seeing one."
"Don't tarry now."
"And be particular 'bout them eggs."
"I have you know my reputation precedes me."
"Unless you can show you a fox, I'll not accord you nothing!"
"He sho' use a heap o' words."
"That has got to be adequate proof."
"You just an ol' confidencer."

Don't tarry now.

Don't be late! Hurry!

Big City Tales

How would *Flossie & the Fox* be different if the setting were somewhere other than rural Tennessee? Pose this question to your students to get them thinking, and writing, creatively! First, draw a chart on the board and label the first column and first row as shown. As a class, complete the "Rural Tennessee" column with information from the book. Then have students brainstorm details for each row in the "Big City" column.

Next, direct each student to refer to the chart as he writes a "Big City" version of *Flossie & the Fox*. Remind him to include a clear beginning, middle, and end. Provide time for each child to read his completed story aloud. Then display the stories on a bulletin board titled "Big City Tales."

	Rural Tennessee	Big City
Character #1	Flossie	Rachel, Robert
Character #2	fox	rat, stray dog
Action	Flossie delivers eggs to a neighbor.	Rachel and Robert deliver newspapers.
Other Animals	rabbit	pigeon
	rat	cat
	cat	mouse
	squirrel	

Sensational Cinquains

Challenge your students to turn Flossie's animal descriptions into diamond-shaped cinquains! To remind students of Flossie's descriptions, reread each one aloud. Next, direct each student to choose one character that Flossie compares to the fox. Provide a sheet of writing paper and guide each child through the steps to create his own cinquain. Direct him to write his words to form a diamond as shown.

Steps:
1. For the first line, write the animal's name in the center of your paper.
2. Write two words that describe the animal for the second line.
3. Think about what the animal does. Write three action words that each end with *-ing* for the third line.
4. Write a four-word phrase about the animal for the fourth line.
5. For the last line, write one word that describes the animal.

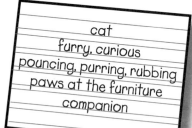

> cat
> furry, curious
> pouncing, purring, rubbing
> paws at the furniture
> companion

Told From a New Voice

When it's time to teach your students about the elements of writing, use this activity to introduce the concept of voice. After sharing the book aloud, explain to students that the voice of a piece of writing refers to the way the author's voice comes through. To get students thinking about the voice of *Flossie & the Fox,* help them identify its distinguishing characteristics, such as humor, dialect, and excitement.

> One day my grandma asked me to take some eggs over to Mrs. McCutchin's house. Mrs. McCutchin lives down the road. I decided to take the quickest path through the woods behind our house. Before I left, Grandma said, "Watch out for that fox! He may want those eggs!"

Next, read aloud the author's note from the beginning of the book. Discuss with students how Patricia McKissack's background plays a part in the voice of the story *(originally told aloud, from the rural South, told with dialect)*. Challenge students to imagine how voice of the story would be different if it were written by another author. To prompt their thinking, ask questions such as the following: Would the story sound different if it were told by me? How would the word choice be different? How would my background affect the way I would tell the story? Then, as a class, rewrite the story on chart paper. Once the story is finished, have a student volunteer read it aloud. Lead students in a discussion of the differences between the voice of the original story and the voice of the new story.

Name _____

What Is a Fox?

Answer each question below.
Use books about foxes to help you.

What do foxes look like?

What do foxes eat?

Where do foxes live?

How do foxes behave?

Note to the teacher: Use with "Finding Out About Foxes" on page 53.

Name_____

Alike and Different

Choose an animal from the word bank.
Write its name at the top of the second egg.
In the first egg, write words that describe only a fox.
In the second egg, write words that describe only your animal.
In the middle, write words that describe both animals.

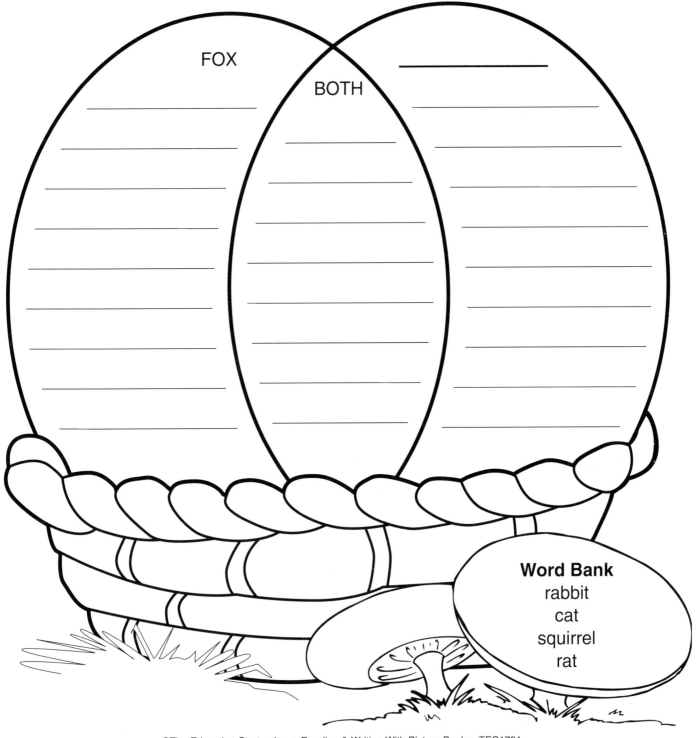

FOX

BOTH

_____

Word Bank
rabbit
cat
squirrel
rat

58   **Note to the teacher:** Use with "Creature Comparisons" on page 54.

Anansi and the Talking Melon

Retold by Eric A. Kimmel
Illustrated by Janet Stevens

Anansi the spider is at it again! After being trapped inside one of Elephant's ripe, juicy melons, he gets bored and decides to trick Elephant into believing that the melon can talk. This irresistible combination of predictability, clever dialogue, and colorful, comical illustrations will have young readers giggling in anticipation of Anansi's next unexpected move!

Character study, story recall

Overheard in the Melon Patch

Who said that? Matching characters with quotes gives students the opportunity to practice their story recall skills! After sharing *Anansi and the Talking Melon* aloud, ask a student to choose one quote from the story. Write the quote on the board, pointing out the capitalization and punctuation in the sentence. Then have other students guess who the speaker is. Repeat this step with several other quotes.

To extend the lesson, give each student a copy of page 63 and provide time for her to complete it.

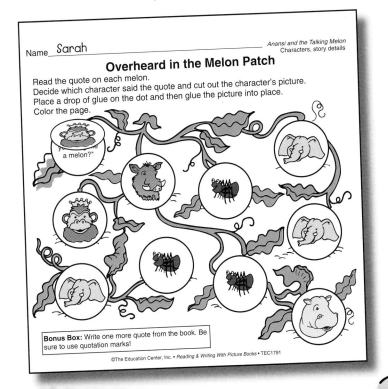

Name Sarah

Anansi and the Talking Melon
Characters, story details

Overheard in the Melon Patch

Read the quote on each melon.
Decide which character said the quote and cut out the character's picture.
Place a drop of glue on the dot and then glue the picture into place.
Color the page.

Bonus Box: Write one more quote from the book. Be sure to use quotation marks!

©The Education Center, Inc. • *Reading & Writing With Picture Books* • TEC1791

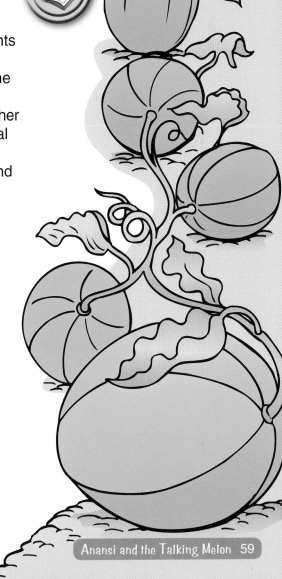

For a Closer Look

Students spin a little character analysis at this "spider-ifc" center! In advance, cut a class supply of four-inch black construction paper circles. In addition, cut eight 1" x 6" black construction paper strips for each child. Display the paper pieces at a center, along with wiggle eyes, glue, white crayons or chalk, and a copy of the book.

Direct each child to write a different word or phrase that describes Anansi on each of his strips. Next, have him glue the strips onto the bottom of the circle to form a spider as shown. After the child labels the spider, have him add wiggle eyes or construction paper eyes to his spider. For an eye-catching display, mount the completed spiders on a bulletin board titled "Take a Look at This Trickster!"

Anansi in Action

Anansi's witty comments and clever actions make this a perfect book for students to retell with puppets. Divide students into groups of five and assign one main character to each group member. Provide assorted craft materials—such as craft sticks, felt, and craft foam—and have each stu-dent make a stick puppet that repre-sents his character.

Next, have the group work together to write a script that retells *Anansi and the Talking Melon*. Direct the group to use its puppets to practice acting out the script. Then allow time for each group to perform its script for the class. If desired, make arrangements with other teachers for each group to visit a neighboring classroom and perform the story.

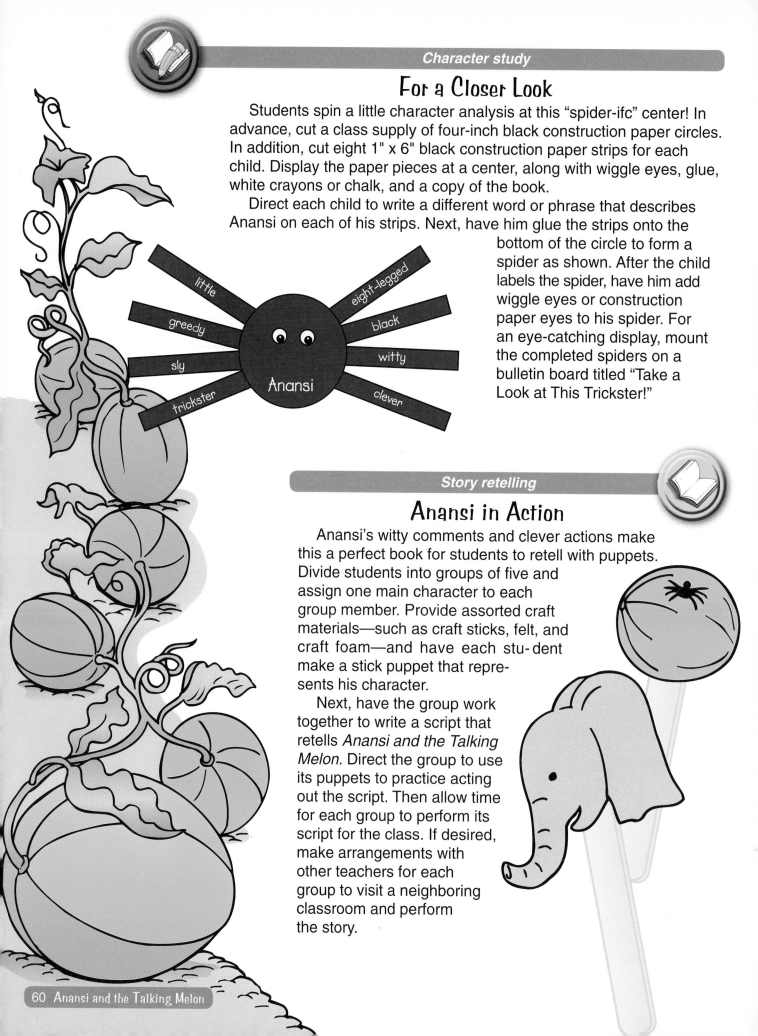

That's Some Spider!

Anansi certainly isn't an ordinary spider. But how much does he have in common with ordinary spiders? Use this fact-or-fiction activity to help students find out! On the board, write the spider descriptions listed below. Explain to students that one of them strictly describes Anansi, one strictly describes real spiders, and one describes both Anansi and real spiders. Ask a different student to read each description aloud, and then have remaining students vote on the type it is. Guide them to conclude that first one describes both, the second one describes Anansi, and the third one describes real spiders.

Next, provide nonfiction spider books as well as a copy of *Anansi and the Talking Melon.* Then give each child two sticky notes. On each note, have him write one thing about Anansi, one thing about real spiders, or one thing about both. In the meantime, draw a Venn diagram on the board and label it as shown. When the sticky notes are completed, invite each child, in turn, to read his notes aloud and then place them on the appropriate circle in the diagram.

Spider Descriptions
1. has eight legs
2. can speak, talks to other animals
3. may live in human homes and eat insect pests

Anansi Real
Both Spiders

Dear Anansi

Anansi manages to anger each of the other characters with his melon prank. Hippo turns red, Warthog shakes all over, and poor Elephant is so upset that he vows never to listen to melons again! This letter-writing activity has students giving Anansi advice on being a better friend. Lead students in a discussion of Anansi's actions and their effects on the other characters. Ask questions such as "What did Anansi do that made Hippo and Warthog angry?" and "Why was Elephant upset?"

Next, ask students to imagine that Elephant has decided to write Anansi a letter. Further explain that Elephant wants to give Anansi some tips on how to be a good freind and neighbor so he can avoid making the other animals angry in the future. Have students brainstorm some tips and list each one on the board. Then give each child a sheet of paper and have him pretend to be Elephant as he writes a letter to Anansi. Bind the completed letters into a booklet titled "Advice for Anansi."

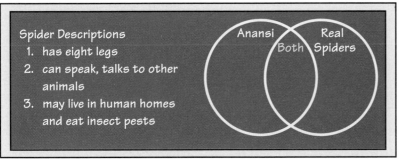

Dear Anansi,

Sincerely,
Elephant

Talking Melons?

Plant the seeds of simile writing with these humorous melon booklets! Provide two eight-inch orange construction paper squares and three eight-inch white construction paper squares for each child. Direct the child to stack her squares so that the orange pieces are on the outside. Give the child a 7½" circle template and have her trace it onto her top orange piece. Next, help her staple the pieces together as shown. Then have her cut out the resulting shape and set her booklet aside.

Explain to students that a simile is a phrase that compares two things using the words *like* or *as.* Reread the section in *Anansi and the Talking Melon* that describes Elephant's meeting with Hippo and Warthog on the road. Point out that the author uses a simile when she compares the idea of a talking melon to a skinny hippo and then to a handsome warthog.

Next, write "A talking melon is as ridiculous as..." on the board. Ask students to name the three nonspeaking characters in the book (Ostrich, Rhino, and Turtle), and list each one on the board. Explain to each student that on each white page of her booklet, she will write a humorous simile for a different nonspeaking character. Then have her illustrate her book, write her name on the front, and title it "Talking Melons?" Be sure to set aside time to share, as students are sure to enjoy hearing each other's humorous similes!

A talking melon is as ridiculous as a cuddly rhino.
A talking melon is as ridiculous as a graceful ostrich.
A talking melon is as ridiculous as a speedy tortoise.

Talking Melons?

Justine

A talking melon is as ridiculous as a graceful ostrich.

Going Bananas Over Writing

Writing a sequel to *Anansi and the Talking Melon* is sure to bring lots of "a-peel" to creative writing! To set the scene, reread the end of the book to students. Next, ask student volunteers to make predictions about the situations that could occur with Elephant and a talking banana. To focus students' thinking, pose questions such as "Would Elephant tell anyone else about the banana, or would he decide to keep it to himself?" and "Would Anansi ever be revealed as the voice behind the fruit?"

As a prewriting activity, give one copy of the graphic organizer on page 64 to each child. Instruct her to fill in the page with her ideas for a sequel. Then have her refer to the page as she writes a sequel to the book. Showcase the stories by mounting each one on a banana bunch–shaped cutout and stapling it to a bulletin board titled "Anansi and the Talking Banana."

Name _____

Overheard in the Melon Patch

Anansi and the Talking Melon
Character study, story recall

Read the quote on each melon.
Decide which character said the quote and cut out the character's picture.
Place a drop of glue on the dot and then glue the picture into place.
Color the page.

"I'm not going to listen to a word you say!"

"You don't have one like this. This melon talks."

"Who said that? Did you say that, Elephant?"

"Elephant will be coming back soon. It is time to go."

"We talk all the time. The trouble is, you never listen."

"Did you say that, Elephant? Did you say that, Hippo?"

"I'm not the one who talks to melons!"

"Why did you bring me a melon?"

"Say whatever you like. I only want to hear you talk."

"I didn't know melons could talk."

Bonus Box: Write one more quote from the book. Be sure to use quotation marks!

©The Education Center, Inc. • *Reading & Writing With Picture Books* • TEC1791

Note to the teacher: Use with "Overheard in the Melon Patch" on page 59.

63

Graphic Organizer

Use with "Going Bananas Over Writing" on page 62.

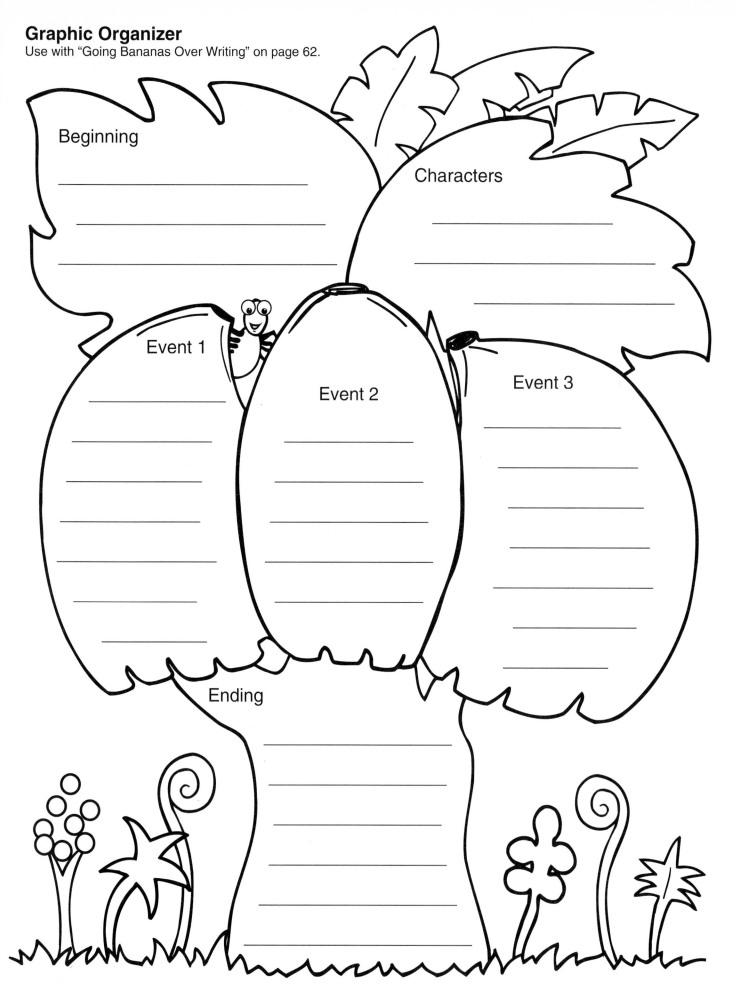

Beginning

_____
_____
_____

Characters

_____
_____
_____

Event 1

_____
_____
_____
_____
_____
_____
_____

Event 2

_____
_____
_____
_____
_____
_____

Event 3

_____
_____
_____
_____
_____
_____

Ending

_____
_____
_____
_____
_____

Chicken Sunday

Written and illustrated by Patricia Polacco

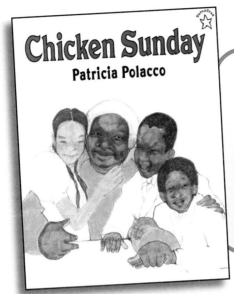

To thank Miss Eula for her years of love and encouragement, three children seek out a way to get the precious Easter bonnet she longs for. Along the way, the children win over the heart of Mr. Kodinski, the hat-shop owner, and share with him their spirit of cooperation and brotherhood.

Explanatory writing, activating prior knowledge

Window Wishes

Before reading the book aloud, give students an opportunity to share what they would do if they needed to earn money. Explain to them that in the story they will be studying, three friends try to find a way to earn enough money to buy the hat their "gramma" sees in a store window. Give each child a sheet of drawing paper and instruct her to draw and color a picture of an item that she would like to purchase for herself or for someone special. On the back of the paper, have her write an explanation of the things she could do to earn money to buy the item. Then have the child complete her window by using construction paper scraps to make curtains on either side of the drawing of the item. Provide time for each child to share her work with the class before mounting her completed paper on a bulletin board titled "Window Wishes." Finally, read the book aloud, instructing students to listen carefully for the things the children do to earn the money they need. Students may be delighted to find that they have some of the same moneymaking ideas that Miss Eula's special grandchildren have!

Getting an aquarium will be easy if I can follow a few simple steps.
_____
_____
_____

Order Up!

These colorful, three-dimensional egg projects are just what you need when you're looking for an activity that inspires students to practice sequencing events! In advance, enlarge the pattern on this page and use it to make several tagboard templates. In addition, write the sentences on this page on the board. Then provide each student with the listed materials and guide him through the steps to make a three-dimensional egg project.

Sentences
The children make Pysansky eggs for Mr. Kodinski.
Mr. Kodinski gives the hat to the children.
The children count the money in their Band-Aid tin.
The children sell eggs in Mr. Kodinski's store.
Some big boys throw eggs at Mr. Kodinski's door.

Materials for one egg:
access to a tagboard egg
    template
5 sheets of 9" x 12"
    construction paper
scissors
glue

Directions for one egg:
1. Use the template, scissors, and construction paper to make five egg-shaped cutouts.
2. Write a different sentence on each egg.
3. Arrange the eggs in sequential order.
4. Fold each egg in half vertically so that the writing is on the inside.
5. In order, glue the back of one-half of each egg to the back of half of the next egg until you have a three-dimensional egg as shown.

Pattern

Elemental Eggs

Looking for an activity to assess your students' understanding of specific story elements? Try this colorful idea! First, review the book with students. Remind them that a story can be developed through its setting, plot, and characters. Then challenge students to name settings, plot events, and characters found in *Chicken Sunday*. Finally, to determine individual understanding, give a copy of page 69 to each child and have him complete the page as directed.

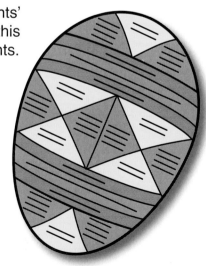

Scrambled Eggs

This "eggs-cellent" activity helps students develop their sentence-ordering skills! In advance, gather six resealable plastic bags and then trim a supply of 2" x 3" construction paper pieces into egg shapes. Program each egg with a different word or punctuation mark from the sentences on this page. As you program the eggs for each sentence, in turn, tuck them into one of the bags. Seal the bag and then program it with a different number from 1 to 6.

Next, divide students into six groups and give each group a bag and enough writing paper for each child to have one sheet. Direct each group to unscramble the cutouts to form a sentence. Have each group member record the bag's number along with the completed sentence on his paper. Then instruct the group to scramble the cutouts, return them to the bag, and pass the bag to the next group. Continue in this manner as time allows.

> Miss Eula loves to look at the hats in the shop window.
> The children want to buy Miss Eula the Easter bonnet.
> Some boys throw eggs at the back door of Mr. Kodinski's shop.
> The children take a basketful of decorated eggs to Mr. Kodinski.
> The children sell their beautiful eggs at Mr. Kodinski's hat shop.
> Miss Eula gets her bonnet from the children on Easter Sunday.

Hats Off to Paragraph Writing!

Here's a top-notch activity that will have students thinking about paragraphs. In advance, program an overhead transparency with the topic sentence shown. After reading the book aloud, ask students to recall how Mr. Kodinski feels about the children when they first visit his shop. *(He is angry because he thinks they threw the eggs.)* Next, ask them to describe Mr. Kodinski's feelings about the children at the end of the book. *(He thinks they are good children.)*

Reveal the programmed transparency and have a student volunteer read the topic sentence. Ask students to brainstorm supporting details that tell them that Mr. Kodinski's opinion changes as you list each one on the transparency. Then give a sheet of writing paper to each child. Have the child refer to the information on the transparency as he writes a paragraph. To publish his work, have the child glue his completed paragraph in the center of a 9" x 12" sheet of construction paper. Then have him trim the construction paper into the shape of a hat as shown. Post the hats on a bulletin board titled "Hats Off to Mr. Kodinski!"

Topic sentence: Mr. Kodinski changes his opinion of the children.

Supporting details:
1. He invites them for tea.
2. He lets them sell their eggs in the shop.
3. He gives them the hat.

Contrasting Characters

Mr. Kodinski and Miss Eula are two very different people, yet by the end of the story they feel the same way about the children. Reread the book aloud to remind students of the diversity of these characters. As you're reading, pause at appropriate points to ask students questions such as "How do you think Mr. Kodinski feels about the children at this point?" or "How is Miss Ella showing her love for the children?" Encourage students to support their answers with examples from the text or details from the illustrations. After reading, have each student take a closer look at the characters by having him complete page 70.

Ending punctuation, writing complete sentences

Get Cracking!

This "eggs-citing" center is sure to provide Grade A ending-punctuation practice for your students! Ahead of time, gather eight plastic eggs. Enlarge the list of questions and answers from this page and then cut the sentences apart. Insert each strip into a different egg. Place the eggs in a basket and set the basket at a center stocked with paper, pencils, and a copy of the book.

At the center, a student opens each egg and reads the sentence. She then sorts the sentences into questions and answers and matches each question with its corresponding answer. Finally, on a sheet of writing paper, the student records each pair of sentences with the correct capital letters and punctuation marks.

Questions	Answers
what does miss eula want	she wants an easter bonnet from mr. kodinski's shop
what does miss eula fix every sunday	miss eula fixes fried chicken after church
how do the children earn money for miss eula's hat	they sell decorated eggs
what does mr kodinski think the children did to his shop	he thinks they threw eggs at the back door

©The Education Center, Inc. • *Reading & Writing With Picture Books* • TEC1791

they sell decorated eggs

Name _____

Decorating With Story Elements

Read the words on the egg.
Color by the code.

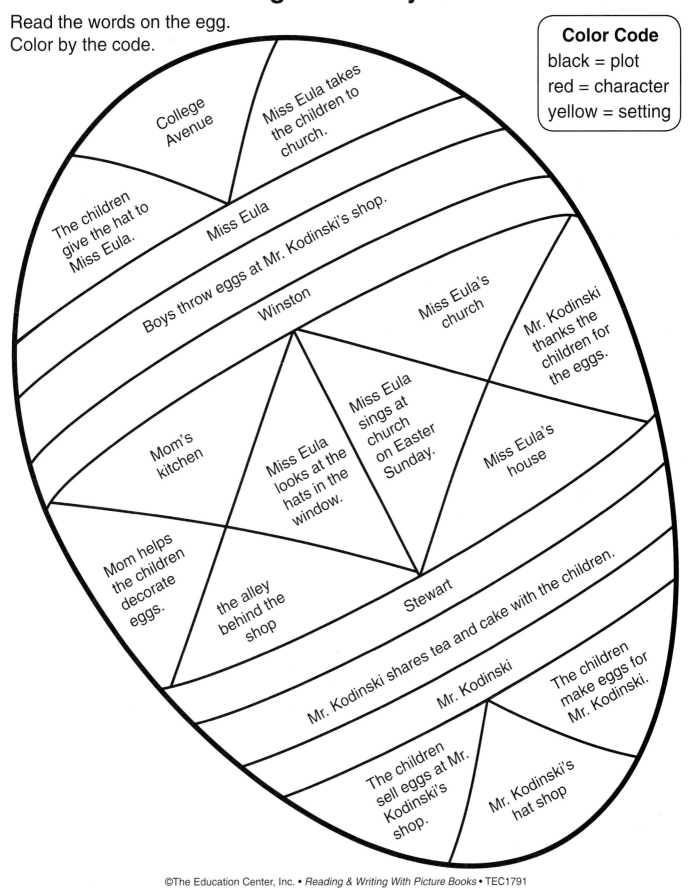

College Avenue

Miss Eula takes the children to church.

The children give the hat to Miss Eula.

Miss Eula

Boys throw eggs at Mr. Kodinski's shop.

Winston

Miss Eula's church

Mr. Kodinski thanks the children for the eggs.

Mom's kitchen

Miss Eula looks at the hats in the window.

Miss Eula sings at church on Easter Sunday.

Miss Eula's house

Mom helps the children decorate eggs.

the alley behind the shop

Stewart

Mr. Kodinski shares tea and cake with the children.

Mr. Kodinski

The children make eggs for Mr. Kodinski.

The children sell eggs at Mr. Kodinski's shop.

Mr. Kodinski's hat shop

Note to the teacher: Use with "Elemental Eggs" on page 66.

Name _____

Character Clues

Read each phrase.
Decide which character(s) the phrase describes.
Cross out the correct egg.

Miss Eula   Mr. Kodinski   Both

1. has had a hard life   A   E   S

2. know the children are good people   T   I   C

3. help the children   H   R   Y

4. has raised the children to be truthful   S   B   E

5. accuses the children of something they didn't do   O   D   H

6. sings in the church choir   K   C   N

7. are pleased by the children's actions   G   R   S

8. has a mean look   K   H   D

9. takes care of the grandchildren   A   E   W

10. receive a special gift from the children   Y   L   N

11. has a voice like slow thunder and sweet rain   I   A   S

12. has a changed heart about the children   N   U   C

What do the children call the afternoons after church?

To answer the question, write the matching letter from each sentence above on the numbered blanks below.

__ __ __ __ __ __ __ __ __ __ __ __ __ __
2 8 11 2 6 1 10 4 12 10 5 9 3 7

Note to the teacher: Use with "Contrasting Characters" on page 68.

It Could Always Be Worse

Retold and illustrated by Margot Zemach

A peasant father has had enough of the noise in his overcrowded hut, so he heads to the rabbi for a little advice. The rabbi tells the man to bring the farm animals, one at a time, into the hut. This results in even more chaos and confusion! Luckily, the rabbi's wise suggestions lead the man to realize how fortunate he really is.

Journal writing

Dear Diary

Encourage students to step into the story with these character diaries! To prepare, make enough copies of the diary page pattern on page 75 for each child to have three. Distribute the pages, and give each child a 9" x 12" sheet of construction paper and one copy of the cover pattern on page 75. Instruct the child to fold her construction paper in half horizontally, tuck the stacked diary pages inside, and then staple along the fold to create a booklet. Have her color and cut out the cover pattern and then glue it onto her diary's cover.

Next, read the first page of the book aloud. Guide the class in a discussion of the feelings each person in the hut may be having. Then ask each student to imagine that she is one of the children living in the hut. Have her open her diary to the first page and write an entry as if she were that child. Provide time for each child to complete her entry.

Resume reading the book aloud through the page that describes life in the hut after the man brings the goat inside. Ask each child to turn to the second page of her diary and write a second diary entry. Encourage her to put herself in the child's place and imagine what the child must be feeling at this point in the story as she writes. After each child has finished her entry, read the remainder of the book aloud. Then have each child turn to the third page in her diary and write a final diary entry. When all students have finished, invite interested children to share their work with the class. As your students get a firsthand look at the story, they'll also get a lesson in perspective!

Dear Diary,

It sure is crowded in here. Everyone is arguing, and there is no place for me to go. The baby cries all the time. I just wish I could get some peace and quiet.

Maria

A New Outlook on an Old Hut

The size of the hut doesn't change, and the number of people living in the hut doesn't change, but the description of life in the hut certainly changes! Invite students to compare the two descriptions with this quick antonym activity! Remind students that antonyms are words that have opposite meanings. Reread the first page and the last two pages of the story aloud.

Next, have students brainstorm antonym pairs that describe the hut at the beginning of the book and the hut at the end of the book as you list their suggestions on the board. For an enriching wrap-up, have students write sentences with pairs of antonyms from the list.

crowded—roomy
noisy—quiet
chaotic—peaceful
sad—happy

In the beginning, the hut is crowded, but later the hut feels roomy.

Chaotic Effects

Each time the poor unfortunate man changes the number of animals living in the house, his action affects the family. Give students the opportunity to explore these cause-and-effect relationships more closely with this charming hut project! After rereading the book aloud, give each child the materials listed below and guide him through the steps to complete the activity.

Materials:
copy of page 76
9" x 12" sheet of white construction paper
scissors
glue
crayons

Steps:
1. Lightly color the hut, avoiding the areas with text.
2. Carefully cut each window and door flap along the dotted cut lines. (Ask for assistance as necessary.)
3. Carefully fold each flap back along the bold fold line as shown.
4. Glue the hut onto the construction paper, being careful not to glue the flaps down
5. Read the cause statement on the top flap.
6. Fold the flap back and write a sentence or more telling what happens as a result of the cause.
7. Continue in this manner with each of the remaining flaps.
8. If desired, use your crayons to add details such as a sky and grass to the scene.

It Could Always Be Worse

Name _James_

Descriptive Dwellings

The walls of this three-dimensional hut are papered with descriptions of scenes in the book! To begin, reread the book aloud. As you're reading, pause to ask questions such as "What do you think the people in the hut are hearing?" and "What do you think the family is seeing in the hut?" After reading, give each child a copy of page 77. Instruct the child to decide which part of the story he would like to focus on. Then have him complete each sentence with his observations of the scenes from the chosen part of the story.

Next, have the child cut out the project along the bold lines, and help him fold each dotted line. Have the child assemble the hut by gluing the project where indicated. Provide time for each child to share his work with the class before taking his hut home to share with his family.

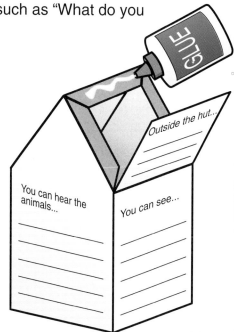

Full House

Use this unique story-mapping activity to teach students to remember details from the beginning, middle, and end of the book! In advance, draw an outline of a three-level house on chart paper and label it as shown. To begin, display the first three two-page spreads, in turn, as you read the text aloud. Ask students to name events and details from the beginning of the book as you list each item in the top chart section.

Then resume reading through the point when the cow has been living in the hut for "some days or a week." Have students name events and details from the middle of the book as you list each item in the middle chart section.

Finally, read the rest of the book aloud. Ask students to name events and details from the end of the book as you list their ideas in the bottom chart section. Display the completed story map for a top-to-bottom reference for the events from the beginning, middle, and end of *It Could Always Be Worse*.

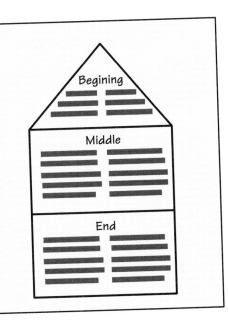

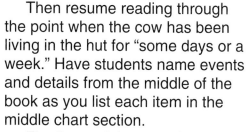

Seeking Advice

Use the rabbi's creative solution to inspire your students to write a letter *and* do a little problem solving of their own! To remind students of the poor unfortunate man's problem, reread the first page of the story aloud. Ask students to brainstorm other solutions to the man's problem, such as telling the man to build an expensive new house or have his children sleep in the barn. Then lead them in a discussion of the rabbi's solution. Guide them to conclude that his solution is indeed very clever and creative.

Next, have students brainstorm problems that they face in the classroom, such as losing pencils, choosing line leaders, and keeping desks tidy. On the board, write a letter to the rabbi describing one of the problems and asking for his advice, as shown. Give each child a sheet of writing paper. Direct him to imagine that he is the rabbi as he writes a letter offering a solution for your problem. Bind the completed letters into a booklet titled "Dear Rabbi."

> Dear Rabbi,
>
> Things are in a bad way with us and getting worse. Every day the students keep losing more and more pencils. We can't find them anywhere! I'm running out of pencils to give them. Help me, Rabbi. I'll do whatever you say.
>
> Sincerely,
> Mrs. Thomas

> Dear Mrs. Thomas,
>
> I think you should give one student the job of pencil keeper. He could collect the pencils and sharpen them every day. Each time someone needs a sharp pencil, she'll have to report to the pencil keeper and trade in her old one. This way, everyone will always have a pencil!
>
> Sincerely,
> Rabbi

Crowded With Words

This wordy learning center has your students searching for nouns, action verbs, and adjectives. Place a supply of writing paper and a copy of the book in the center. Instruct each child to fold his paper in thirds and then unfold it to create three columns. Have him label each column with a different heading, as shown. Next, have him read the book and search for words to write in the appropriate columns. Once the child has recorded 15 words in each column, invite him to use the list as a word bank. Have him refer to his word bank as he writes sentences about the story on a second sheet of writing paper.

Nouns	Action Verbs	Adjectives
village	lived	poor
man	fought	unfortunate
mother	lived	six
wife	argued	little

Dear Diary,

diary cover

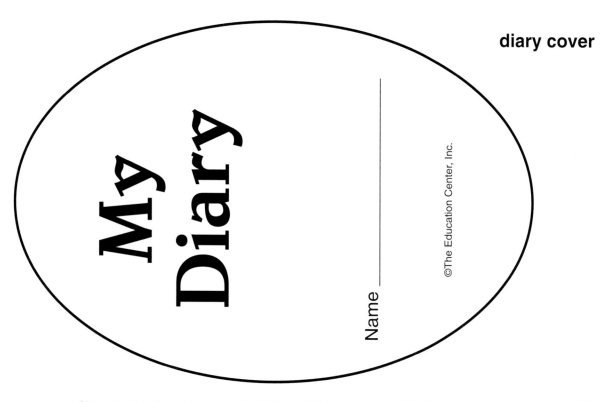

My Diary

Name _____

©The Education Center, Inc.

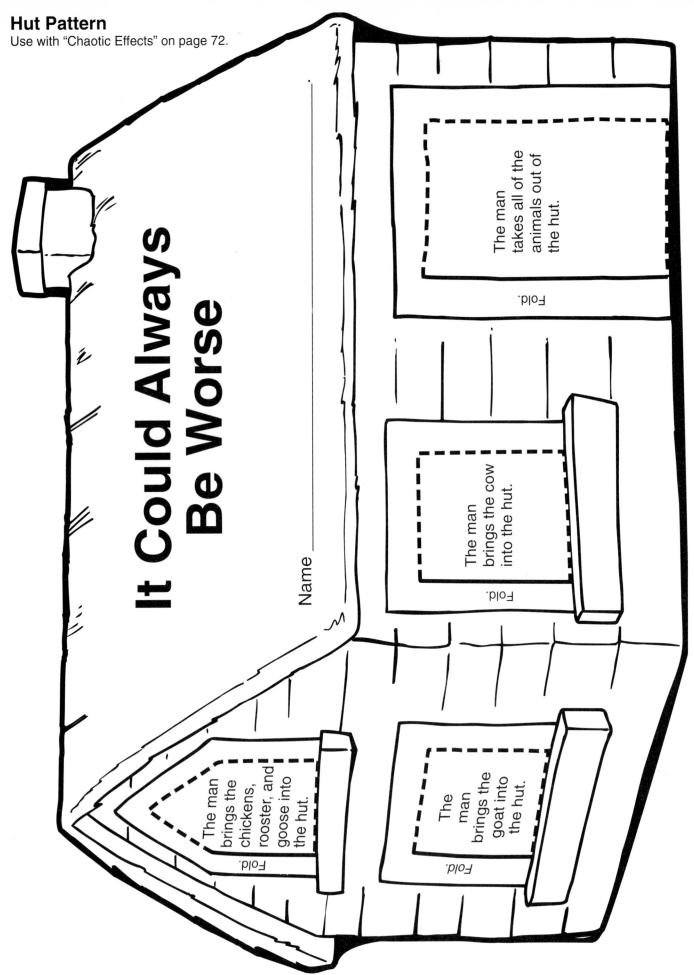

It Could Always Be Worse

Name

The man takes all of the animals out of the hut.

Fold

The man brings the cow into the hut.

Fold

The man brings the chickens, rooster, and goose into the hut.

Fold

The man brings the goat into the hut.

Fold

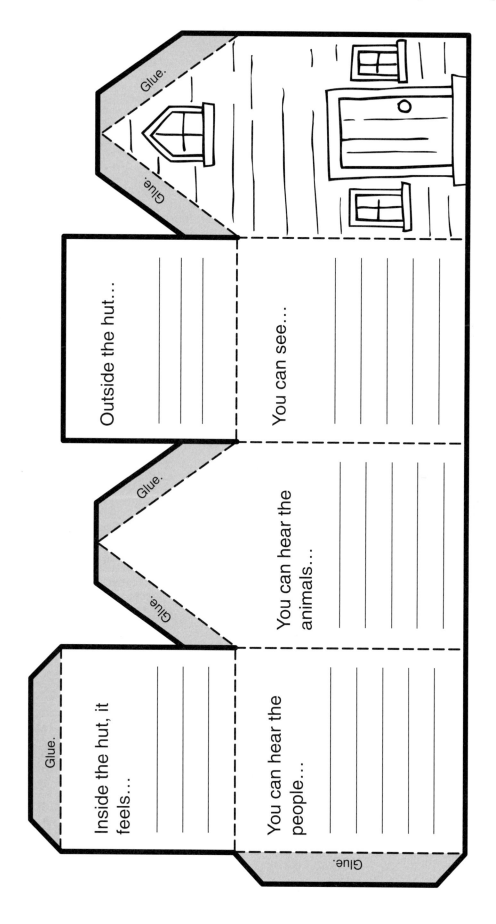

Glue.

Glue.

Glue.

Glue.

Glue.

Glue.

Glue.

Outside the hut...

You can see...

You can hear the animals...

Inside the hut, it feels...

You can hear the people...

Reading Skills Chart

Skill	Tacky the Penguin pp. 5–10	Bringing the Rain to Kapiti Plain pp. 11–16	Frog and Toad Are Friends pp. 17–22	Tops & Bottoms pp. 23–28	Amazing Grace pp. 29–34	Sheila Rae, the Brave pp. 35–40	Today Was a Terrible Day pp. 41–46	Alexander and the Wind-Up Mouse pp. 47–52	Flossie & the Fox pp. 53–58	Anansi and the Talking Melon pp. 59–64	Chicken Sunday pp. 65–70	It Could Always Be Worse pp. 71–77
activating prior knowledge		●		●	●		●		●		●	
answering higher-level questions								●				
antonyms		●	●									●
beginning, middle, and end												●
cause and effect				●			●					●
character study	●		●		●	●				●	●	
comparing and contrasting									●			
comparing and contrasting characters	●											
conflict and resolution	●								●			
distinguishing fact from opinion					●							
distinguishing reality from fiction								●		●		
dramatization						●						
main idea and supporting details								●				
point of view			●									
sequencing events			●	●							●	
setting						●						
story elements							●				●	
story recall				●	●	●	●			●		
story retelling										●		
using context clues									●			
using rhyme and rhythm to predict text		●										
vocabulary	●							●	●			

Writing Skills Chart	Tacky the Penguin pp. 5–10	Bringing the Rain to Kapiti Plain pp. 11–16	Frog and Toad Are Friends pp. 17–22	Tops & Bottoms pp. 23–28	Amazing Grace pp. 29–34	Sheila Rae, the Brave pp. 35–40	Today Was a Terrible Day pp. 41–46	Alexander and the Wind-Up Mouse pp. 47–52	Flossie & the Fox pp. 53–58	Anansi and the Talking Melon pp. 59–64	Chicken Sunday pp. 65–70	It Could Always Be Worse pp. 71–77
adjectives	●											
cause and effect		●										
character study				●								
creative writing	●	●				●	●		●	●		
descriptive writing	●		●						●			
developing sentence structure											●	
ending punctuation		●									●	
explanatory writing					●						●	
friendly-letter writing			●				●					
journal writing												●
letter writing										●		●
main idea and supporting details						●						
narrative writing				●	●			●				
paragraph writing				●			●				●	
parts of speech												●
persuasive writing								●				
poetry writing			●	●				●	●			
punctuating dialogue							●					
responding to literature					●							
sequencing events		●										
setting	●								●			
similes										●		
story elements					●							
story recall												●
writing complete sentences	●	●									●	
writing compound sentences		●										
writing proper nouns						●						
writing with voice									●			

Answer Keys

Page 9

1. e
2. c
3. d
4. h
5. g
6. f
7. a
8. b

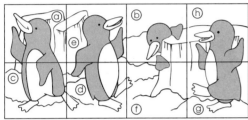

Page 28

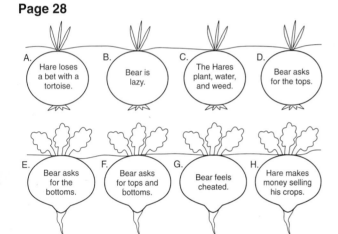

A. Hare loses a bet with a tortoise.
B. Bear is lazy.
C. The Hares plant, water, and weed.
D. Bear asks for the tops.
E. Bear asks for the bottoms.
F. Bear asks for tops and bottoms.
G. Bear feels cheated.
H. Hare makes money selling his crops.

Page 46

1. "Why do you look like a snake under that table?" asked Miss Tyler.
2. Miss Tyler asked, "Why are you eating Jimmy's sandwich in the closet?"
3. "I forgot to have my mother sign my homework," said Ronald.
4. Ronald asked, "Can you help me with my workbook page?"
5. "I hope I get to go to third grade," said Ronald.
6. "You need to look at that word again," said Miss Tyler.
7. Ronald said, "I knocked the plant off the windowsill."
8. "I wish I could read as well as Billy," thought Ronald.
9. Miss Tyler said, "I think you can read this note by yourself."

Page 51

	Real	Make-Believe
1. Every time they see Alexander they chase him with a broom.	✓	
2. Alexander hears a squeak in Annie's room.	✓	
3. "Who are you?" asks Alexander.		✓
4. Alexander and Willy become friends.		✓
5. One day Willy tells a strange story about a magic lizard.		✓
6. The lizard tells Alexander to bring him a purple pebble.		✓
7. Annie is going to throw Willy away.	✓	
8. Alexander sees a purple pebble.	✓	
9. There is a full moon.	✓	
10. The lizard changes Willy into a real mouse.		✓
11. Alexander runs back to the house as fast as he can.	✓	
12. Alexander and Willy dance until dawn.		✓

Bonus Box: Answers will vary.

Page 70

1. E
2. C
3. Y
4. S
5. D
6. K
7. S
8. H
9. A
10. N
11. I
12. U

CHICKEN SUNDAYS